THE
TOMMY
COOPER
JOKE BOOK

Also by John Fisher

Funny Way to be a Hero
The Magic of Lewis Carroll
Call Them Irreplaceable
George Formby: The Ukulele Man
Never Give a Sucker an Even Break
Paul Daniels & the Story of Magic
Body Magic
Cardini: The Suave Deceiver
Tommy Cooper: Always Leave Them Laughing
Tony Hancock: The Definitive Biography

THE TOMMY COOPER JOKE BOOK

Compiled by JOHN FISHER

preface

Published by Preface 2009

10 9 8 7

First published in Great Britain in 2009 by Preface Publishing
20 Vauxhall Bridge Road
London, SW1V 2SA

An imprint of The Random House Group Limited

www.rbooks.co.uk
www.prefacepublishing.co.uk

Addresses for companies within The Random House Group Limited
can be found at www.randomhouse.co.uk

The Random House Group Limited Reg. No. 954009

A CIP catalogue record for this book is available from the British Library

ISBN 978 1 84809 198 6

The Random House Group Limited supports The Forest Stewardship Council (FSC),
the leading international forest certification organisation.
All our titles that are printed on Greenpeace-approved
FSC-certified paper carry the FSC logo.
Our paper procurement policy can be found at www.rbooks.co.uk/environment

Designed and artworked by Andy Spence Design
www.andyspence.co.uk

Printed and bound in Great Britain by
MPG Books Ltd, Bodmin, Cornwall

In memory of Max Miller...

...the Pure Gold of the Music Hall

Best Wishes
Tommy Cooper
TOMMY
COOPER
BILL
HALL

CONTENTS

1.	INTRODUCTION	1
2.	'LADIES AND GENTLEMEN, TOMMY COOPER...'	26
3.	TOMMY'S CHILDHOOD	30
4.	TOMMY'S LAUGHTER PRESCRIPTION	34
5.	TOMMY AT THE SEASIDE	37
6.	TOMMY AND HIS DOG	39
7.	COOPER'S LAUGHTER ALLSORTS	42
8.	TROOPER COOPER	44
9.	COOPER'S FEZ TALES	47
10.	TOMMY IN THE JUNGLE	48
11.	HOMAGE TO MAX MILLER	50
12.	MEET THE WIFE	54
13.	TOMMY DREAMS	59
14.	TOMMY'S ONE-LINERS	62
15.	TOMMY ON STAGE	64
16.	TOMMY AND HIS AGENT	66
17.	TOMMY GOES DOWN MEMORY LANE	68
18.	COOPER'S HECKLER STOPPERS	69
19.	TOMMY'S EARLY STAND-UP	72

CONTENTS

20. Cooper's Pub Tales 76
21. Cooper Classic 1 78
22. Tommy's Lucky Dip 79
23. Musical Cooper 80
24. Philosophical Cooper 82
25. Meet the Family 86
26. Tommy at the Dentist 89
27. Cooper à la Carte 90
28. Unlucky For Tommy 92
29. Stating the Obvious 94
30. Tommy the Boxer 101
31. Cooper Classic 2 105
32. Back with the Audience 106
33. Cooper's Animal Crackers 109
34. Tommy and the Law 112
35. More laughter Allsorts 115
36. Tommy Goes Abroad 116
37. Risqué Cooper 118
38. Cooper Classic 3 121

39. More One-Liners 122
40. Courting Cooper 123
41. Back at the Doctor's 124
42. Back in the Jungle 127
43. The Most Famous Man in Britain 128
44. Encore for maxie! 130
45. Cooper Classic 4 133
46. Tommy Goes Shopping 134
47. Meet the Wife Again 136
48. Tommy the Film Star 140
49. Cooper the Poet 142
50. More Lucky Dip 143
51. Tommy at the Wheel 145
52. Cooper Classic 5 147
53. Cooper by Royal Command 148
54. The Hats Routine 149
55. A Last Roundup 164
56. Acknowledgements 166

'HERE'S A QUICK JOKE. I WANT TO HEAR IT MYSELF!'

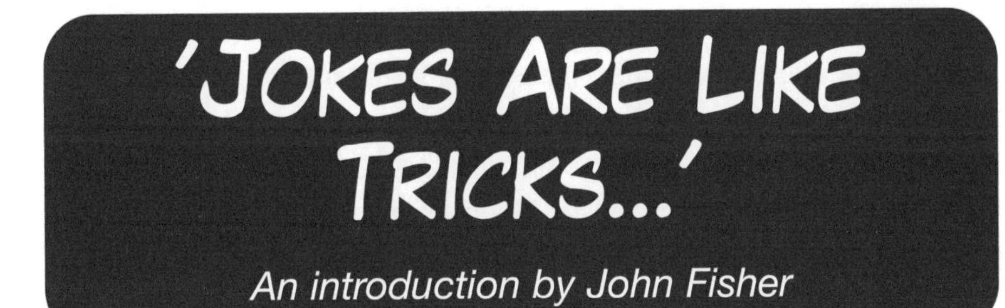

'Jokes Are Like Tricks...'

An introduction by John Fisher

It is twenty-five years since Tommy Cooper died the most visible of deaths live on television on the stage of Her Majesty's Theatre in London's West End. Unwittingly a showman till the end, he kept the audience in suspense as his gangling bulk crumpled beneath a voluminous scarlet and gold lamé cloak in the manner of the master stage illusionists of his youth. Visually it seemed the prelude to the most spectacular of vanishing tricks and he would have relished the expectation that fell upon the audience before the grim reality dawned. In the same way he would have loved the hint of contradiction in that first sentence. One can hear him now proclaiming, 'Dead, live. Live, dead.' He had a way with words – teasing their meaning, relishing their ambiguity, falling foul of their pitfalls – in a manner that was as joyous as his way with the pedestrian props of the magician's trade. 'Egg, bag. Bag, egg.' 'Bottle, glass. Glass, bottle.'

No one who saw or heard Cooper ever forgot him and since his death the status of folk hero he acquired in his lifetime has become raised to an even higher level as new generations have caught up with his comedy through technology that once would have appeared to be real magic. It is well documented how Tommy took his first step on the road to acclaim as the world's most successful worst wizard, when the milk in the bottle refused to defy the law of gravity at a concert he gave in a works canteen when a shipyard apprentice just outside Southampton in his late teens. After the initial sting of disappointment, the not-displeasing sound of laughter that then greeted his misfortune had a life-transforming effect on him. Magic tricks began to be chosen with their built-in laughter potential in mind. More importantly jokes and gags that did not need props soon became grist to the comedic mill, not least when war called and the scope for entertaining his army chums was restricted by his inability to carry anything but the lightest of magical apparatus in his kitbag. His stage shows would follow the pattern of tricks and gags – 'Gag, trick. Trick, gag' – until the end of his days.

Ironically, although everyone has a favourite memory of Cooper attempting to purvey his hocus-pocus craft, what people remember most affectionately about him are the funny lines that, whatever their origin, needed only him to say them to be stamped with his copyright for evermore. It seemed, therefore, an appropriate way to mark the silver anniversary of his death to compile this volume. While not pretending to be encyclopaedic, it represents a comprehensive anthology of most of his familiar stand-up material and much else besides. I almost wrote 'familial' there and one is reminded that the original meaning of the earlier word was one of just such family intimacy. The jokes themselves have become old friends and achieve their greatest effect when told – preferably with a Cooper voice and Cooper gestures – amongst near ones and dear ones, the safest short-cut to hilarity at a family dinner table at celebratory times of the year. Cooper's radiant warmth and instant rapport as a performer informed his telling of them and I am sure that in any poll of recent entertainers whom the public at large might wish to invite to such a gathering, he would come in miles ahead of the rest of the pack. Not that Cooper could have been any card but the Joker, the rightful court jester in a monarchy where, as these pages will show, he entranced both the ruler and her subjects.

By contrast, away from the spotlight and the public gaze, Cooper was a serious man. To watch him fret over the fine detail of an exploding piece of magic apparatus or worry over the disposition of the crazy props on his

'SUCCESSFUL JOKES ARE CONTAGIOUS AND BECOME MODIFIED IN THE PASSING AND THIS HAS PROBABLY BEEN SO SINCE THE BEGINNING OF TIME.'

table just before he sauntered on stage was to discern a perfectionist that might have put Fred Astaire to shame. His attitude to comedy was no less punctilious, although it surprises many people to discover that he did not write his own material – at least not the ninety-nine per cent that failed to qualify as instant ad-lib forged in the heat of performance and seldom paraded again until the same circumstances prevailed. Today performers on the comedy circuit are to a large extent regarded as *persona non grata* if they are not recognised as the originators of their material. In Tommy's time everyone took for granted that Bob Hope had a battalion of joke writers and that Tony Hancock was a lesser animal when deprived of a Galton and Simpson script. And yet so intense and persuasive was the persona of the genial fez-capped zany that people assumed automatically that he was a creative genius – which he was, of course, but in other ways entirely.

Within his own resources the young Cooper went to extreme lengths to ensure that nothing missed his attention. He was introduced to joke-book culture as a performer through the slender pamphlets written by Robert Orben, a slick American comedy writer who happened also to be a professional magician. These slender tomes could be picked up readily over the counters of the best magic shops in London. Many of the lines were linked to established magic tricks, many were stand-alone one-liners. The booklets in their gaudy soft paper covers flaunted themselves under titles like 'Patter Parade', 'Laugh Package', 'Bits, Boffs and Banter' and 'Screamline Comedy.'

To a top professional funny man the outlay of fourteen shillings was considered a sound investment if only one workable gag was forthcoming from the pages purchased. However, the popularity of the books within the comedy profession led to the over-familiarity of much of their contents. Lenny Bruce once advertised a performance with the tag line, 'No Joe Miller (a reference to the morose eighteenth century actor whose name became synonymous with stale humour), no corn, no Orben.' Orben threatened to sue, though never did. In his later years he would become speech writer to President Gerald Ford, providing a quirky footnote to American political history in a way that none of his comedy customers of the forties and fifties could have envisaged.

Tommy soon realised he needed something a little more exclusive and in the early fifties found the solution on a visit to New York where he became acquainted with Billy Glason, an ex-vaudevillian who had travelled America with an act billed as 'Just Songs and Sayings.' To keep boredom at bay on the relentless circuit away from home, old pros notoriously turned to booze, broads, or golf. Glason was the exception and appears to have kept himself out of mischief by compiling on index cards files of every joke he ever heard. When he retired from the stage, he set to and began to reorder this material, often twisting and adapting it to keep pace with the times. Ed Sullivan, Johnny Carson, Steve Allen, even Bob Hope began to avail themselves of his services. Tommy found himself to be the lucky Briton in the right place at the right time, one of the privileged few granted purchase of Glason's gargantuan twenty-six part 'Fun-Master Giant Encyclopaedia of Classified Gags.' In the days before photo-copying became commonplace, the material was published on the thinnest paper possible, 'to make it possible to make as many carbon copies as we can!' What Glason lost on the number of copies, however, his purchasers made up for in exclusivity. The work is reputed to have been advertised originally for three thousand dollars, although the paperwork in Cooper's files shows that he paid a knockdown price of nine hundred. It was still a lot of money over fifty years ago.

Over the next few years Tommy acquired much more from Glason, including the five volumes of his 'Book of Blackouts', the three of his 'Book of Parodies', the nine lessons of his 'Comedy and Emcee Lecture Book', not to mention his 'Humor-Dor for Emcees and Comedians.' In bulk this material, all published under Glason's 'Fun-Master' imprint, must approximate to the combined capacity of the accumulated telephone directories amassed by the average individual in a couple of lifetimes. Cooper also subscribed to a monthly sheet issued by Billy entitled simply 'The Comedian.' Similar bulletins of gag material were issued by two more New Yorkers, Art Paul's 'Punch Lines' and Eddie Gay's 'Gay's Gags.' The British scriptwriter Peter Cagney followed suit with his own newsletter. They all fell through the Cooper letter box. To peruse his copies today is tantamount to being perched on his shoulder as he scrupulously read each gag and marked those that appealed accordingly. Not that the marks predominate. There was just so much to choose from.

Tommy's favourite bedtime reading.

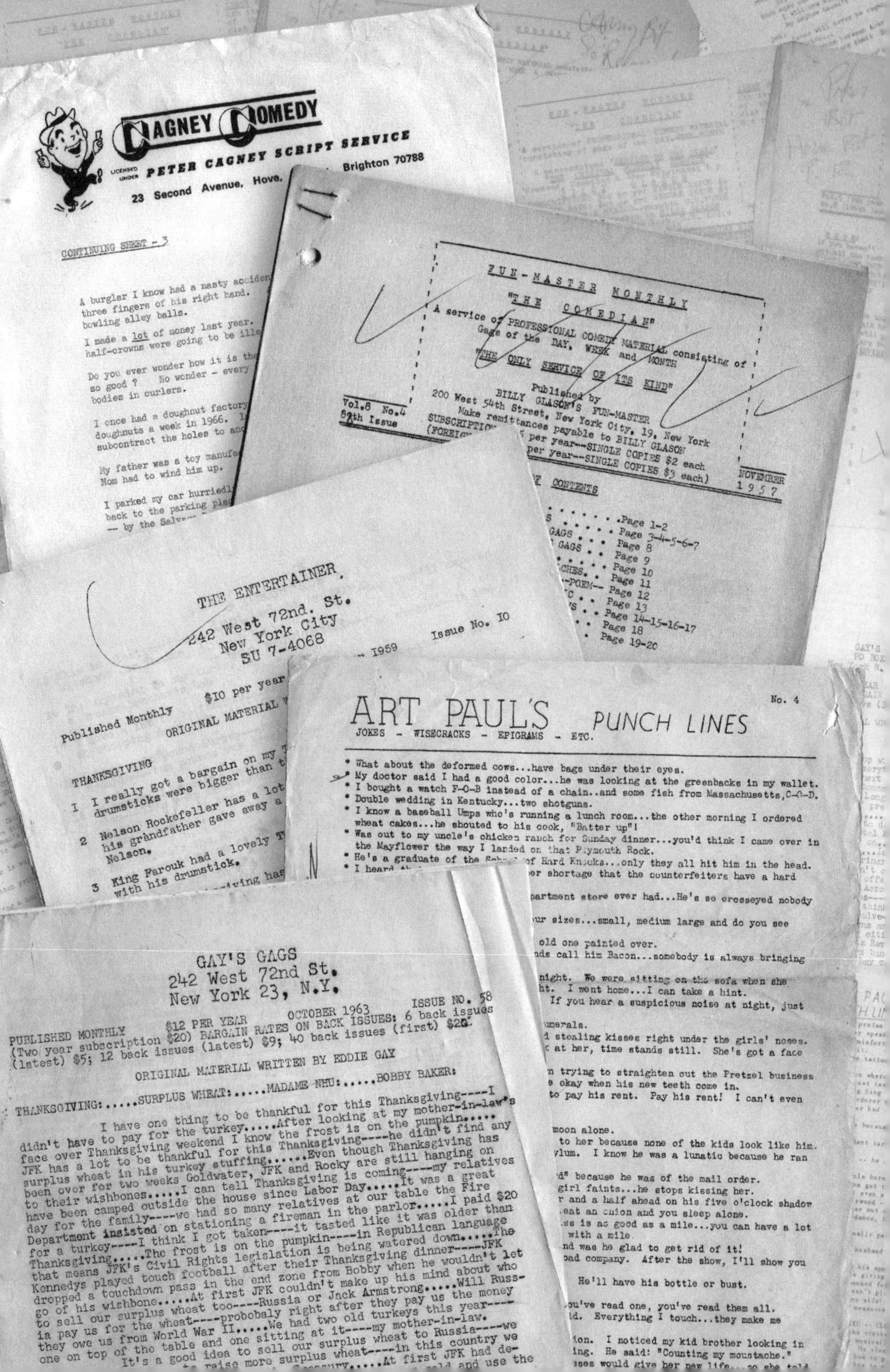

CAGNEY COMEDY

PETER CAGNEY SCRIPT SERVICE

LICENSED UNDER

23 Second Avenue, Hove, ... Brighton 70788

CONTINUING SHEET - 3

A burglar I know had a nasty acciden... three fingers of his right hand. ... bowling alley balls.

I made a lot of money last year. ... half-crowns were going to be ille...

Do you ever wonder how it is th... so good ? No wonder - every ... bodies in curlers.

I once had a doughnut factory ... doughnuts a week in 1966. I... subcontract the holes to an...

My father was a toy manufa... Mom had to wind him up.

I parked my car hurriedl... back to the parking pla... -- by the Salv...

FUN-MASTER MONTHLY

"THE COMEDIAN"

A service of PROFESSIONAL COMEDY MATERIAL consisting of Gags of the DAY, WEEK and MONTH

"THE ONLY SERVICE OF ITS KIND"

Published by BILLY GLASON'S FUN-MASTER

200 West 54th Street, New York City, 19, New York

Make remittances payable to BILLY GLASON

SUBSCRIPTION ...5 per year--SINGLE COPIES $2 each

(FOREIG... per year--SINGLE COPIES $3 each)

Vol.8 No.4

8?th Issue

NOVEMBER 1957

... CONTENTS

...S . . . . . .Page 1-2

...GAGS . . . . Page 3-4-5-6-7

... GAGS . . Page 8

... . Page 9

...CHES. . . Page 10

...-POEM-- Page 11

... Page 12

...TC . . Page 13

...S . . Page 14-15-16-17

... . . Page 18

... Page 19-20

THE ENTERTAINER

242 West 72nd. St.

New York City

SU 7-4068

Issue No. 10

... 1959

Published Monthly $10 per year

ORIGINAL MATERIAL W...

THANKSGIVING

1 I really got a bargain on my T... drumsticks were bigger than t...

2 Nelson Rockefeller has a lot ... his grandfather gave away a ... Nelson.

3 King Farouk had a lovely T... with his drumstick.

ART PAUL'S PUNCH LINES

No. 4

JOKES - WISECRACKS - EPIGRAMS - ETC.

* What about the deformed cows...have bags under their eyes.
* My doctor said I had a good color...he was looking at the greenbacks in my wallet.
* I bought a watch F-O-B instead of a chain..and some fish from Massachusetts,C-O-D.
* Double wedding in Kentucky...two shotguns.
* I know a baseball Umps who's running a lunch room...the other morning I ordered wheat cakes...he shouted to his cook, "Batter up"!
* Was out to my uncle's chicken ranch for Sunday dinner...you'd think I came over in the Mayflower the way I landed on that Plymouth Rock.
* He's a graduate of the School of Hard Knocks...only they all hit him in the head.
* I heard th... ...per shortage that the counterfeiters have a hard

...partment store ever had...He's so crosseyed nobody

...ur sizes...small, medium large and do you see

... old one painted over.

...nds call him Bacon...somebody is always bringing

...night. We were sitting on the sofa when she ...ht. I went home...I can take a hint.

If you hear a suspicious noise at night, just

...umerals.

...d stealing kisses right under the girls' noses.

... at her, time stands still. She's got a face

...n trying to straighten out the Pretzel business

...e okay when his new teeth come in.

... to pay his rent. Pay his rent! I can't even

...moon alone.

... to her because none of the kids look like him.

...ylum. I know he was a lunatic because he ran

...d" because he was of the mail order.

... girl faints...he stops kissing her.

...r and a half ahead on his five o'clock shadow

...eat an onion and you sleep alone.

...s is as good as a mile...you can have a lot with a mile.

...nd was he glad to get rid of it!

...oad company. After the show, I'll show you

He'll have his bottle or bust.

...ou've read one, you've read them all.

...d. Everything I touch...they make me

...ion. I noticed my kid brother looking in

...ing. He said: "Counting my moustache."

GAY'S GAGS

242 West 72nd St.

New York 23, N.Y.

PUBLISHED MONTHLY $12 PER YEAR OCTOBER 1963 ISSUE NO. 58

(Two year subscription $20) BARGAIN RATES ON BACK ISSUES: 6 back issues (latest) $5; 12 back issues (latest) $9; 40 back issues (first) $20

ORIGINAL MATERIAL WRITTEN BY EDDIE GAY

THANKSGIVING:.....SURPLUS WHEAT:.....MADAME NHU:.....BOBBY BAKER:

I have one thing to be thankful for this Thanksgiving----I didn't have to pay for the turkey.....After looking at my mother-in-law's face over Thanksgiving weekend I know the frost is on the pumpkin..... JFK has a lot to be thankful for this Thanksgiving----he didn't find any surplus wheat in his turkey stuffing.....Even though Thanksgiving has been over for two weeks Goldwater, JFK and Rocky are still hanging on to their wishbones.....I can tell Thanksgiving is coming----my relatives have been camped outside the house since Labor Day.....It was a great day for the family----we had so many relatives at our table the Fire Department insisted on stationing a fireman in the parlor.....I paid $20 for a turkey----I think I got taken----it tasted like it was older than Thanksgiving.....The frost is on the pumpkin----in Republican language that means JFK's Civil Rights legislation is being watered down.....The Kennedys played touch football after their Thanksgiving dinner----JFK dropped a touchdown pass in the end zone from Bobby when he wouldn't let go of his wishbone.....At first JFK couldn't make up his mind about who to sell our surplus wheat too----Russia or Jack Armstrong.....Will Russia pay us for the wheat----probobaly right after they pay us the money they owe us from World War II.....We had two old turkeys this year---one on top of the table and one sitting at it----my mother-in-law. It's a good idea to sell our surplus wheat to Russia----we ... raise more surplus wheat----in this country we ...

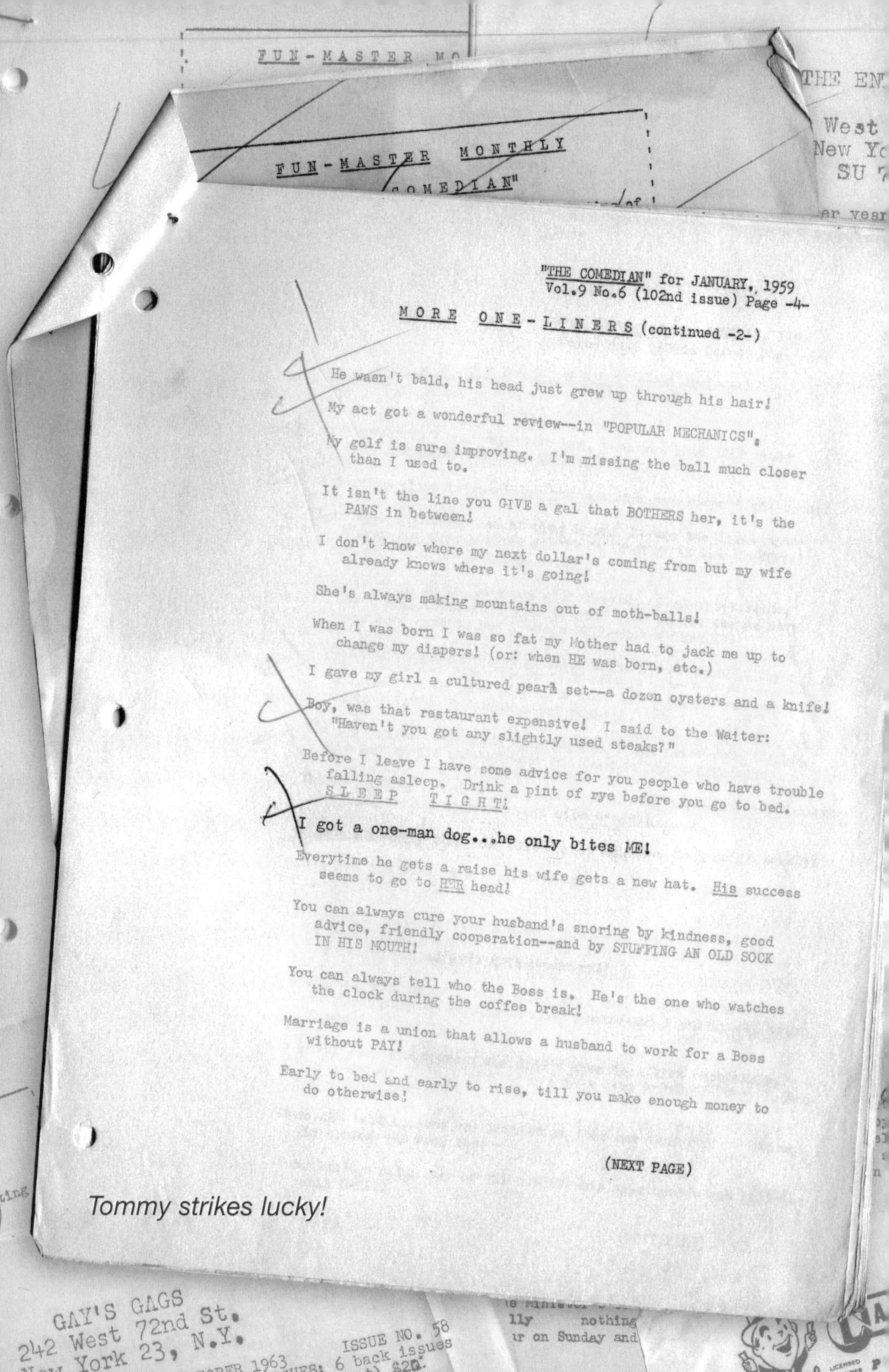
"THE COMEDIAN" for JANUARY, 1959
Vol.9 No.6 (102nd issue) Page -4-

MORE ONE-LINERS (continued -2-)

He wasn't bald, his head just grew up through his hair!

My act got a wonderful review--in "POPULAR MECHANICS".

My golf is sure improving. I'm missing the ball much closer than I used to.

It isn't the line you GIVE a gal that BOTHERS her, it's the PAWS in between!

I don't know where my next dollar's coming from but my wife already knows where it's going!

She's always making mountains out of moth-balls!

When I was born I was so fat my Mother had to jack me up to change my diapers! (or: when HE was born, etc.)

I gave my girl a cultured pearl set--a dozen oysters and a knife!

Boy, was that restaurant expensive! I said to the Waiter: "Haven't you got any slightly used steaks?"

Before I leave I have some advice for you people who have trouble falling asleep. Drink a pint of rye before you go to bed. SLEEP TIGHT!

I got a one-man dog...he only bites ME!

Everytime he gets a raise his wife gets a new hat. His success seems to go to HER head!

You can always cure your husband's snoring by kindness, good advice, friendly cooperation--and by STUFFING AN OLD SOCK IN HIS MOUTH!

You can always tell who the Boss is. He's the one who watches the clock during the coffee break!

Marriage is a union that allows a husband to work for a Boss without PAY!

Early to bed and early to rise, till you make enough money to do otherwise!

(NEXT PAGE)

Tommy strikes lucky!

They always tell you to be ready when Opportunity knocks!. Well, one night I was ready, when somebody knocked and spoiled a beautiful opportunity!

Why do they rave so much about Marilyn Monroe? Take away her sexy look and her terrific figure and what have ya got? MY WIFE!

Even though he's wealthy now he's never forgotten his poor childhood on the lower East Side. Once a month he goes back there to visit his wife and kids!

When I asked her to have something to eat, she said "I file for a great big steak, what do YOU file for?" I said "I file for bankruptcy!"

I told the waiter the cup was dirty and he said "You're crazy, that's not dirt, that's only lipstick!"

I just had a BOY SCOUT COCKTAIL--two of them and an old lady helps YOU across the street!

When I gave my kid a pony for his birthday, he said "What IS it, a FOREIGN HORSE?"

She's on a diet of cocoanuts and bananas. She hasn't lost any weight but Boy, can SHE climb TREES?

When people tell me I'm growing old, I remind them that I still chase pretty young girls. The only difference is now that I chase them I can't remember why I started CHASING them!

(NEXT PAGE)

laugh at HUNTLEY & BRI...

I enjoy Las Vegas because everybody out there gambles. One day I went into a drug store for some aspirin and the Druggist said "I'll flip ya double or nothing!" I wound up with TWO HEADACHES!!

Her mother sings in a quartet. She's the BASS SINGER!

(NEXT PAGE)

...she wore a white dress. I thought she was a REFRIGERATOR!

She was too ugly to have her face lifted so they lowered her body instead!

(continued)

Cooper set a high standard, knew exactly what he was looking for and compiled a more compact A – Z index of his own. In fact, only a small percentage of what he highlighted as suitable corresponds to the material that became most associated with him down the years. Tommy always claimed that the hardest part of his television shows was pulling together his stand-up spots, which were mostly deemed his responsibility, as distinct from the sketches written by top comedy writers of the day and his mangled magic tricks, which to an extent chose themselves once he had been seduced by them in the heady atmosphere of the magic depots he loved frequenting. Needless to say, there was never a problem in having enough material in the end. Cooper may have thought he was subscribing to a joke service; but, in effect, the masses of paper that piled high in the Cooper home provided another service, acting as the lucky talisman against the day when his tried and tested stuff was taken away from him and audiences stopped laughing. The nightmare was an occupational hazard for any comic.

The exact pedigree of much of what Orben, Glason and the others purveyed is lost to history. Jokes often seem to be born without conception. We can recognise a joke as an old joke, but when we are honest with ourselves we are unlikely to have heard it before (unless it is an accepted favourite in an act like Cooper's, in which case we are disappointed when we don't hear it again) and are unable to pinpoint a source. But as Gershon Legman, the legendary chronicler of scatological humour, limericks, origami folds (sic) and much else besides, wrote, 'Nobody ever tells jokes for the first time.' The exaggeration contains a basic truth. Successful jokes are contagious and become modified in the passing and this has probably been so since the beginning of time.

At the very least Cooper stands as a colossus at a pivotal time in the oral tradition of jokes. He was indisputably the exemplar of the contagion process as applied to comedy. No British comic of recent times has been quoted by an adoring public more extensively for its own amusement than he has been, in a way that is tantamount to an extension of his own performance. Things also worked in reverse. Back in his early days jokes seemed to circulate far more freely amongst the profession, comics appropriating from one another with impunity, in a way that the more watchful ethos of the television and DVD era does not allow. A telling one-liner from the early part of his career went, *'Now get ready for this one – it's one of the first jokes I ever stole.'* When I asked Tommy's widow, Gwen – always known to him as 'Dove' – to identify for me the source of a particular piece of business he had featured in his act, she replied, 'I think we saw that in Vegas. We nicked it, like we nicked everything else!' Actually they didn't nick or steal anything, at least no more than anybody else, or Billy Glason.

Aside from the reams of purchased material that Tommy perused with dedicated attention, his quickly established reputation in British show business attracted comedy material from much nearer to home. His files overflow with submissions – mostly unsolicited – not only of jokes, but monologues, parodies, sketches, and comedy magic scenarios. Few ever saw the light of day on stage or screen. However, three names tower above the rest in any overview of his stand-up material and deserve recognition here. They are Val Andrews, Freddie Sadler, and Eddie Bayliss. Bayliss was a lorry driver by profession whose submissions fitted Cooper so magnificently that he was soon signed up by Tommy's agent to secure a hold on his services, although it does not appear that he ever totally gave up his day job. To Bayliss we owe, *'My feet are killing me – every night when I'm lying in bed they get me right round the throat like that'* and many other Cooper gems. Eddie also provided Tommy with one of his most precious visual comedy bits on the occasion of a Royal Gala before the Queen. Cooper took a sword from his table and with one eye on the Royal Box carefully laid it on the ground. He knelt expectantly behind it for a few telling seconds, during which nothing happened. Then he got up, reclaimed the weapon and shrugged, *'Well, you never know, do you?'* Even the Queen laughed.

'WELL,
YOU NEVER KNOW,
DO YOU?'

Sadler's letterhead reveals that he was a 'Comedy Impressionist and Compère' on the London concert party circuit during the early fifties. His flair for one-liners was less spectacular than that of Bayliss, although fans should nod obeisance whenever they hear the line, *'Here we have a skipping rope – so we'll skip that!'* More importantly, amid many suggestions for misguided magic for Tommy's early television career, he co-devised with Val Andrews the single most memorable non-magical sequence in the performer's repertoire, the one with 'the Hats.' Val was a versatile individual who juggled the performing and selling of magic with comedy scriptwriting and the writing of Sherlock Holmes pastiches. Their joint creation, which began as an idea from Andrews and to the bones of which each subsequently added flesh, is immortalised in Cooper lore and while not a joke or series of jokes per se, calls out for inclusion in any book on Cooper's humour and will be found towards the end of these pages. It is doubtful if the pair ever received remuneration equal to the true worth of the routine and it is proper that Andrews and Sadler should be accorded proper credit here.

Whatever the source of his material, Cooper had an unerring ability to spot what would work for him. He once pinpointed what he was looking for when he explained that the two most important devices in comedy were a surprise and a funny picture. Unsurprisingly the following pages represent a surreal cartoon gallery of the unexpected: *'I slept like a log last night. I woke up in the fireplace.'* Most jokes are like magic tricks, deriving their energy from twists in logic or language or both, in the way that the art of conjuring takes liberties with the accepted realities of the world. A definitive Cooper gag has qualities of conciseness, and an outrageous courting of the obvious that might seem to contradict the surprise theory. However, Tommy, as a magician himself, knew that the most effective mysteries depended upon the simplest methods. However familiar audiences became with the outrageous literalism of so much of his wordplay, they never saw it coming, even when they had heard the joke several times before. It is appropriate that, as a man who with his bulk, grotesque features and jubilant raucousness embodied so many of the physical attributes of Mr Punch, he approached punch lines with an abandon that rendered the obvious momentarily invisible. Such is the misdirection of the great magician, as in, *'Sometimes I drink my whiskey neat. Other times I take my tie off and leave my shirt hanging out.'* Jerry Seinfeld has drawn a parallel between telling a joke and jumping over a metaphorical canyon with the audience coming along for the ride. No comic ever made the shortness of the gap more exhilarating than Cooper.

Freud famously said that jokes needed to convey their message not just in a few words, but in too few words. The manuscript records of his material that Cooper left behind reveal how he refined individual gags over the years, honing and polishing them to haiku-style intensity. Here Tommy is talking of his childhood early in his career:

I'll never forget the time I was doing a trick in the living room before an open fire – my father came home and almost killed me – we didn't have any fireplace!

This became:

One day I was doing tricks in front of a big fire. My father came in and hit me. We didn't have a fireplace!

One day I was doing tricks in front of a big fire. My, father came in and hit me – we didn't have a fireplace!!...

Sometimes one longer joke would in the course of time do more effective service as two. The topic is his wife:

One morning she got up with curlers in her hair, cream all over her face, wearing an old dressing gown and she went to take the rubbish out – and when she saw the rubbish lorry moving away, she said, 'Hey, am I too late?' and the dustman said, 'No, lady, jump in!'

This evolved into the double whammy of:

She ran after the dustman – and said I'm too late for the dustcart? He said – No jump in!!

She puts that cold cream on at night curlers in her hair, then she puts a fishing net over the whole thing. She said – Kiss me. I said, Take me to your leader.

She ran after the dustman and said, 'Am I too late for the dustcart?' He said, 'No – jump in!'

alongside

She puts that cold cream on at night – curlers in her hair – then she puts a fishing net over the whole thing. She said, 'Kiss me.' I said, 'Take me to your leader!'

While Cooper became a past master when it came to brevity, his versatility set him out as an equal exponent of the honourable exception to all the rules, the device that takes perverse delight in delaying the resolution of the final punch line through any number of diversions and digressions. I refer to the shaggy dog story. Dogs seldom figure in them, although in Cooper's case other animals frequented them with amazing regularity. He had a habit of finding himself in the jungle so often that at the risk of paraphrasing Kipling one could refer to these escapades as his *Just Like That* stories, if not exactly his *Just So* ones. Several examples occur in the pages ahead. Cooper's strength was, of course, all in the telling. Where appropriate, I have interpolated his verbal asides and, as virtual stage directions, descriptions of the gestures and mannerisms that enabled him to bring these rambling and potentially boring discourses – together with much more – so hilariously to life.

It has been said of Cooper that many of his jokes could have come out of Christmas crackers. In fact, I have a favourite image of Tommy as Santa Claus, the capacious sack on his back spilling over with magic tricks and jokes – animal jokes, waiter jokes, dog jokes, doctor jokes, policeman jokes, wife jokes. The spirit of play underpinned his work in a childlike way, transporting his audience – temporarily released from the bonds of logic and reality – back to the euphoric state of childhood. Much of this world was the one of *Dandy* and *Beano*, although conversely many of his lines are suggestive of deeper philosophical reasoning, poised between ignorance and a more exalted mental power: *'Somebody once said that horsepower was a very good thing when only horses had it.'* One recalls his apparently simplistic statement that while other people paint apples, bananas and oranges, he paints the juice. As I said in *Always Leave Them Laughing*, my earlier biography of the comedian, such comments acknowledge 'a questioning of the way the world works that gets close to the higher level of conceptual or representational humour exploited so successfully by Spike Milligan in *The Goon Show*, going beneath the level of language to the fundamental structures of thought and life itself.' The frequency with which dream jokes recur in his repertoire is significant here: *'The other night I dreamt I was eating a ten-pound marshmallow. When I woke up the pillow had gone!'* Freud again likened jokes to dreams arguing that in both a topsy-turvy logic holds sway. Cooper was the funniest advocate of the theory. It was a bonus that even at the peak of his form and his physical condition no comedian conveyed a greater impression of sleepwalking through his act.

'WEE WILLIE WINKIE
RUNS THROUGH THE TOWN
UPSTAIRS AND DOWNSTAIRS
IN HIS NIGHTGOWN...
...AND YOU THINK I'M NUTS!'

With Cooper nothing could be taken for granted. Even if the hilarity and festive ambience of his act imparted a safe feeling to his audiences, he could hit a disconcertingly macabre streak. A radio discussion programme once targeted a Tommy Cooper joke as the all-time greatest gag: *'This fellow knocked at a door and said, 'Hello – is Charlie in?' The woman replied, 'Charlie died last night.' The man said, 'He didn't say anything about a pot of paint, did he?'* Whether you find that funny or not – and it has to be admitted that it is closer to Gary Larson's *The Far Side* and *The Addams Family* than the typical Cooper joke – it sums up the futility of life itself, the human condition at literally its most skeletal. Steven Wright, the brilliantly dour American stand-up comedian who has done more than anyone to make existentialism an easy bedfellow of laughter, on one occasion analysed his own humour as 'the thoughts of a child, with an adult voice.' In my career as a television producer I once had the privilege of presenting Wright and Cooper as guests on the same show. Wright came out with lines like, 'Lots of comedians have people they try to mimic. I mimic my shadow' and 'He asked me if I knew what time it was. I said, "Yes, but not right now."' Their mutual respect upon discovering each other was joyous and I wish I could have signed up the visitor to write exclusively for Cooper there and then.

If Tommy knew what he was looking for, he also had self-imposed guidelines on what to avoid. Straightforward insult humour seemed reserved almost totally for his agent, Miff Ferrie, with whom his love-hate relationship has become an established part of recent British show business folklore. As for xenophobia, long a staple of the traditional stand-up, Tommy's joke about the Chinese Jews is purely a linguistic trick and is hostile to no one, while the joke about the Mexican, the Irishman and the German is as innocuous as the one about the three bears and relies as much on its three-part structure as on any latent racism for its humour. He hardly ever went further than that, unless it was the occasion at a Variety Club luncheon in honour of Dean Martin, when he addressed the crowd, 'When you think of Martin and Lewis, it's amazing how things have turned out. Dean Martin has become an international star known all over the world. I often wonder what happened to the Eyetie who did all the singing!' But Tommy had little time for stereotypes. When he wanted to joke about stupidity, he had only to direct the laugh against himself for the biggest response – apart, that is, from his long-suffering wife.

The tradition of the wife joke in the Cooper canon owes as much to his reverence for his boyhood comic hero, Max Miller, as to any aggression towards his partner in marriage, Gwen, for whom, in spite of what the tabloids have voiced to his apparent discredit in the years since his death, he maintained a deep-rooted love to the end of his days. This is not the place for an analysis of the complex emotional triangle of his latter years. The only relevant aspect of their relationship in our context is the advice Gwen, or 'Dove', gave him in his early days, namely that if he ever told a dirty joke on stage, she would divorce him. He more or less kept to that promise, and is on record as saying, 'Once you tell the first dirty joke you tell another and before you know where you are, you've got a blue show and I don't want that. It's very difficult to get back from blue material to clean material.' The nearest he got to the knuckle was on the back of a playground naughtiness, as in the prop gag with the three-cup brassiere – *'I met a funny girl last night!'* – although in scrutinising his comedy files it was perhaps surprising to find that he was not averse to the occasional one-liner that was more risqué – and even in today's climate more politically incorrect – than one obviously associates with him. For the record a selection of them is included here, but essentially you could guarantee the whiteness of your weekly wash by the standard set by Cooper's humour. And as for him taking lines from Maxie like *'I've got the best wife in England. The other one's in Africa!'* Gwen would have no qualms. There wasn't a woman who didn't adore the self-proclaimed Cheekie Chappie in his outrageous plus-fours and technicolour clothes, in spite of any insinuation that he might have been otherwise sexually disposed: 'Well, what if I am?'

In the joke appropriation stakes, no British comic was probably more sinned against than the great Max Miller. Max reigned triumphant as the 22-carat doyen of risqué humour throughout the thirties and the forties, Tommy's formative years. But he was never unsubtle and skilfully left the meaning of what he was saying to the imagination of his audience. Not only Cooper, but every member of his generation keen to ply the trade of comedian on the boards, wanted to emulate him, in awe not only of his daring and bravado,

but his timing and technique. In the latter years of the great comedian's life, the young magician befriended his hero, whom he came to regard as a veritable guardian angel. Although he had no intention of discarding his fez, Tommy treasured Max's trademark white snap-brim trilby, which Miller presented to him. Their verbal styles were totally dissimilar – the one the shrill salty cadences of Brighton's seafront, the other the heavier burr of the West Country – and the full measure of how much Tommy appropriated from the older man's repertoire only became apparent to this writer when I confronted Tommy's notes of the material in question. Although both their repertoires were well known to me, I had not previously acknowledged the duplication, so distinctive had been their two deliveries. But while Tommy may have reworked material first popularised by his mentor, what he more importantly acquired from Max was the special creativity that goes into delivery and interpretation. Tommy's true copyright was in the rhythm and phrasing that all his impersonators have imitated, but which no one can steal in such a way as to claim as their own. It is all about discovering your own voice. Like Miller's, Tommy's delivery, with its emphases and skilled use of repetition, achieved an innate precision – unconscious maybe – that wholly belied the fumbling exterior of the dysfunctional magician.

It is seldom that Cooper comes in for criticism. When he does so, it is often down to the supposed antiquity of his material and his propensity for laughing at his own jokes. With regard to the former, he had no qualms. It all came back to self-belief. He once discussed telling the corniest joke in the world: 'You have to have such innocent faith in it that the audience just has to laugh.' Once Cooper had convinced himself that something was funny, the audience was already halfway to laughter. Billy Glason hit the nail on the head in his sales pitch: 'There are no old gags! The only thing old about old gags are the ones who've heard them before and the answer to those who want to admit their age when they remark that a gag is old, is "Say, you don't look that old!"' Tommy voiced his own feelings on the matter to his fellow magician, David Hemingway: 'It doesn't matter how old the gag is.

It doesn't matter how many times the audience has heard it before. If it's funny, it's funny.' And he was always the professional optimist. It may be that one of the fundamental rules of comedy is not to laugh at one's own jokes. But all rules are set to be broken and nothing enhanced the jokes he was telling more effectively than the distinctive foghorn-cum-chortle of a laugh that resonated at those key moments when he paced his material for maximum effect. There was the added advantage that as a character device it could register fear, nervousness, jubilation or act as supposed cover-up for his own inadequacy. Never did he overuse or misjudge the device. With it he could ride his audience like a surfer rides the waves.

Compiling this book has been helped by the vast accumulation of manuscript material Tommy left behind. He was completely methodical in his madness. When it came to props and magic tricks he never left a single thing to chance, making sure that he had two, sometimes three of everything he needed. Similarly, he seldom performed a show without the security of a cue sheet of tricks and gags sneaked away somewhere amongst the props that overburdened his table. Similarly he wrote out new material in long-hand as a means of fixing the joke and its rhythms in his mind. These cards may occasionally have found their way onto his table top too, although I defy anyone to recall a performance when he would have read from them slavishly. If stacked in a pile the amount of cardboard he used up in the process during his career must have come close to rivalling Nelson's Column. In a pre-recycling age, every single scrap of the material lying waste in the Cooper household was called into service. The sheets of cardboard that came to strengthen new shirts were particularly favoured: there were so many that one wonders if he ever wore the same shirt twice. Postcards, menu cards, even the slim cards that many moons ago were used to separate Shredded Wheat in the box were all called into play. By extracting much of this material from the cards themselves and reproducing it in facsimile, this book attempts to bring the reader closer to Cooper as he set out on the laughter trail.

The first prize will be a free extraction of a tooth of your own choice!!

200lbs. of putty for each member of ...

... Almost New!

Audience Lines

... I feel better, than I look.

... nervous tonight I'm afraid I'll ... funny.

... a Dummy don't worry I've got ...

... you get a dance ...

quiet the ... for laughs.

I had a polaroid camera so that I could get a close up of that ...

And before I go lets have a nice big hand for the boys in the Forces.

I've had some wonderful evenings and this isn't one of them.

Took my wife to the beach
I let her bury me in sand
Then I buried her in sand
Next Summer I'm going to dig her ...

Hotel - 3 o'clock in morning - Man loses his temper ... on door - What did ye ...
Nothing - I just kept ... my drums!

I'd like to say something but I don't like the spell.

Quick Short Stories

Did you enjoy the ride? Yes Mam, and we met the nicest policeman. He stopped the car and said "Daddy a ticket"

Taxi Man - I'll take the kids for nothing. The father ... turned to the kids and said - OK, jump in children, and ... Mam & I will take the ...

Teacher - To a 4 year old ...

He was but a simple
CAP + WRENCH
Who married a lady called
LADY'S HAT with Rose.
He met her by chance, ...

TENNIS RACQUET ...
Whilst mending ...
He got damp ...
And whenever he ...
WALK WITH 'SQUE...
CLOTH CAP + WRE...

T.V.

and I wish you would ...
I've just come back from H'wood - I made two pictures, one like this - the other like that!! I'm proud ...

Gags

When I was a kid I had a cute little button
But they couldn't ...
It was buttoned ...

Lady has a baby every five minutes ... she got to find her and just ... stop

T.V. to it!!

Health card, give or I'll kill you.

don't you going to stay in for the ... Sir?

Opening! - Good ... to me evening!

Random Bits

My wife is crazy ... furs and she wanted something different. She went to a furrier ... crossed a mink with a gorilla. She got a beautiful coat, only the sleeves are too long.

Gypsy fortune teller, who doesn't read the tea leaves She reads the lemon.

Bill Bailey. He's not coming Home.

Two 3 ... my wife - ...

POST CARD

Top hat Riding ...

Doctor

Last night I looked up an old friend - what a terrible sight!!

I spent an hour on the phone with my wife last night - the settee ...

... I stand 15 ...

Any entertainer only succeeds because he or she corresponds to a particular moment in time and, although Cooper was not a topical or satirical comic who spun comedy out of the day's headlines, no attempt has been made in these pages to lose cultural references that may no longer carry the meaning they once did. Timothy Whites, Danish Bacon and Lux soap flakes, dairy queens, home perms and living bras need no other explanation than that they placard the era of his greatest success, even if it is hard to accept – as one joke inherited from Max Miller insists – that there was a time when Chelsea played in the 'second division' and that Cooper began his career when the future of television was less a foregone conclusion than one might have presumed: *'Everybody's saying television is here to stay. I don't know. The Hire Purchase company is taking mine back tomorrow.'* One line not included is the one he often resorted to when he had to pour water in a glass in the cause of a trick. Casting a wary glance at the liquid, he would muse, *'It'll never sell!'* long before the craze for bottled water became a licence for money to flow. One wonders what he would have made of the joke potential lurking within the minutiae of life today. It is not hard to hear him complaining that he couldn't get on the tube because his Oyster wouldn't open and that a Blackberry is a messy way to make a phone call, that the Amazon is a long way to go to buy a book and that he couldn't watch BBC because the Sky's the limit.

Hopefully his fans will derive enjoyment from the following pages and those who missed Tommy in his own lifetime will nevertheless have assimilated from reruns and tribute programmes enough about his voice, physical presence and persona to be able to read the contents with him in mind. I do not expect any reader to burst into laughter at seeing a joke reproduced in the cold context of print on the page, but I do beg people as they read to imagine the laughter that greeted Cooper as he performed it all, whether one-liner, shaggy dog tale, or the more continuous pieces where he was able to edit jokes together in such a way as to achieve a genuine conversational rapport with his audience. Let us not forget that Tommy's very best joke was

the man himself, capable of making audiences laugh at the mere mention of his name. That presence informed his words in a mysterious alchemical way, which even he never understood. He took jokes very seriously indeed, but I am equally sure that he would not have wanted this book to be taken too seriously.

'Ladies and Gentlemen, Tommy Cooper...'

(Tommy enters at start of his act to wild applause)
Thank you very much. Thank you. Now I must say you've been a wonderful audience and now I'm gonna finish with a little song. A little song entitled, 'I can't get over a girl like you, so get out of bed and make the tea yourself.'

You know I can always tell whether an audience is going to be good or bad. *(Sniffs)* Good night!!

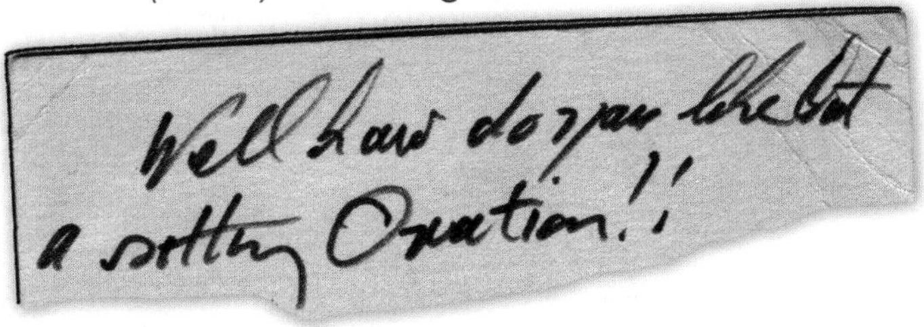

Well how do you like that – a sitting ovation!

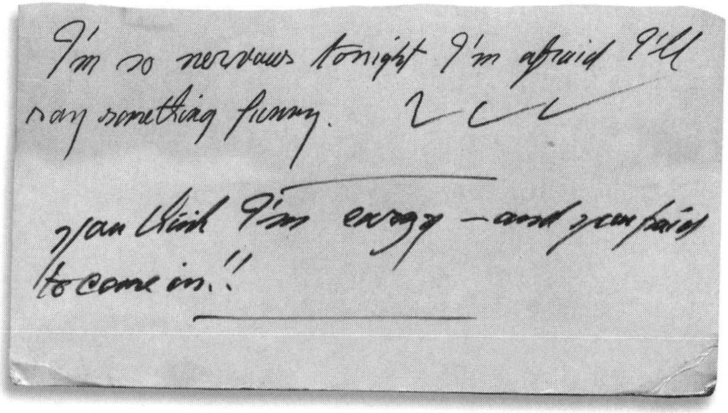

I'm so nervous tonight, I'm afraid I'll say something funny.

You think I'm crazy – and you paid to come in!!

What happened? Somebody else come on?

What a lovely audience – I'll do the full act tonight – I won't cut a thing...

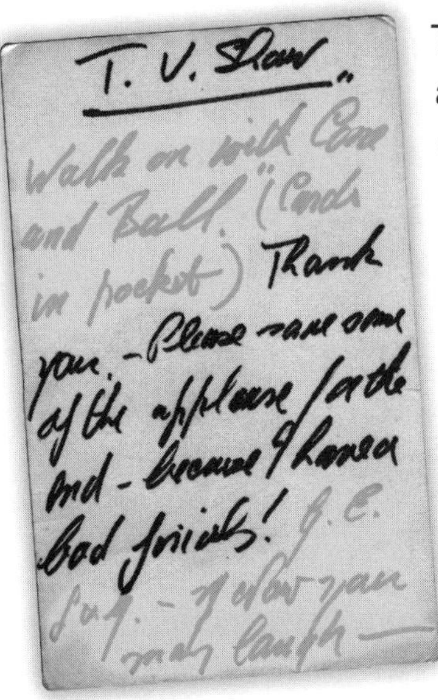
T. V. Show
Walk on with Cane and Ball. (Cards in pocket) Thank you. – Please save some of the applause for the end – because I have a bad finish! T.C.

Thank you. Please save some of the applause for the end – because I have a bad finish!

I don't care what you think. I'm staying in show business!

If you think this weather has ruined your evening, wait until you see my act.

Do you know, I'd give anything to sit out there and watch this!

I have a bit of advice for hungry young Comedians – Eat Something!!

I have a bit of advice for hungry young comedians – eat something.

I spent three years learning judo – I had to – with an act like mine I had to defend myself!

I haven't been on T.V. for a while due to ill health – I make people sick!!

I haven't been on TV for a while due to ill health. I make people sick!!

There was one man in one night. I said, 'Where are you going?' He said, 'I'm leaving.' I said, I'll come with you. I don't want to be on my own.'

I got a letter from my fan club. It said, 'Our membership is swelling. They've all got the mumps!'

Excuse me laughing – you all look so funny out there. You probably all think, what am I gonna do next. I don't know 'what I'm gonna do next.' I really don't!

They told me to have humility and be humble. I've never seen such a humiliating audience in my whole life!

Don't laugh – I feel better than I look.

TOMMY'S CHILDHOOD

Tommy was born on 19 March 1921 in Caerphilly in Wales. When he was three his family relocated to Exeter, where they remained until they moved again to Langley, just outside Southampton, when he reached his teens.

I was born at a very early age – I cried just like a baby.

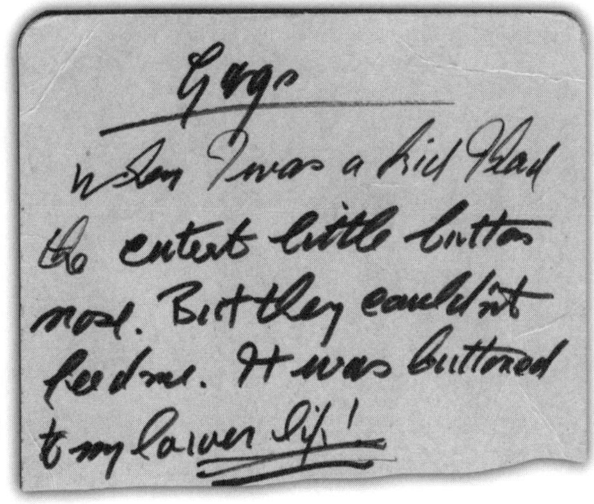

Gags

When I was a kid I had the cutest little button nose. But they couldn't feed me. It was buttoned to my lower lip!

I was a surprise to my parents. They found me on the doorstep. They were expecting a bottle of milk.

When I was a kid I had the cutest little button nose. But they couldn't feed me – it was buttoned to my lower lip.

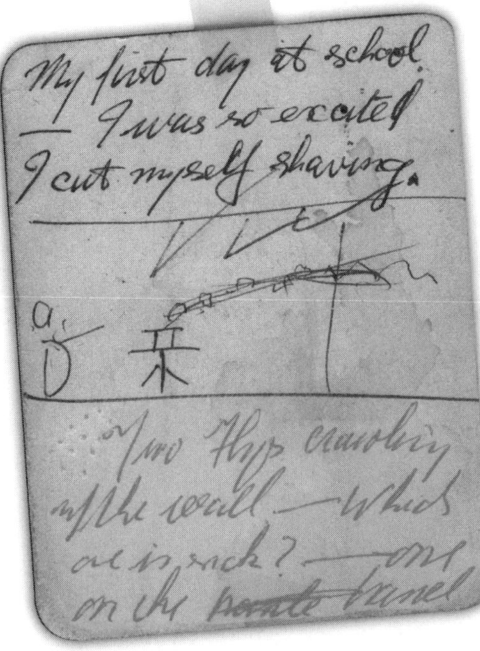

My first day at school I was so excited I cut myself shaving.

My first day at school – I was so excited I cut myself shaving.

Then I grew up! I had to – what other way could I grow?

One day I was doing my tricks in front of a big fire. My father came in and hit me. We didn't have a fireplace!

When I was four years old my father caught me smoking. I'll never forget how he yelled at the kid who set me on fire.

I never had a present for Xmas! My father was a farmer and he use to go outside and fire his gun — and come in and say — Santa Claus has just commited suicide!!

I never had a present for Christmas! My father was a farmer and he used to go outside and fire his gun and come in and say, 'Santa Claus has just committed suicide.'

When the nurse said 'Youve got an 8lb bundle of joy – She said 'Thank God the laundry's back.

When the nurse told my mother that we had an eight pound bundle of joy, my mother said, 'Thank god – the laundry's back.'

I was born with a silver knife in my mouth. My father was a sword swallower!!

I was born with a silver knife in my mouth. My father was a sword swallower!

I was born with a silver spoon in my mouth. When they took it out I was alright.

Even when I was a kid I was always smiling. I swallowed a banana – sideways!

When I was born they thought I was going to be a footballer – because I dribbled on my bib!

When I was two years old I memorised the entire Encyclopaedia Britannica, but no one believed me because I couldn't talk!

I shall never forget my father said to me, 'If you go into show business and disgrace the family, I shall disown you. I won't leave you any money at all.' And I said, 'I don't care, dada.' I did. 'Dada!' So he tried to bribe me. He bought me yachts, motorcars, aeroplanes, a gold studded yoyo, and I said, 'Dada.' I said, 'I don't want material things. I want love and affection. Get me a blonde!'

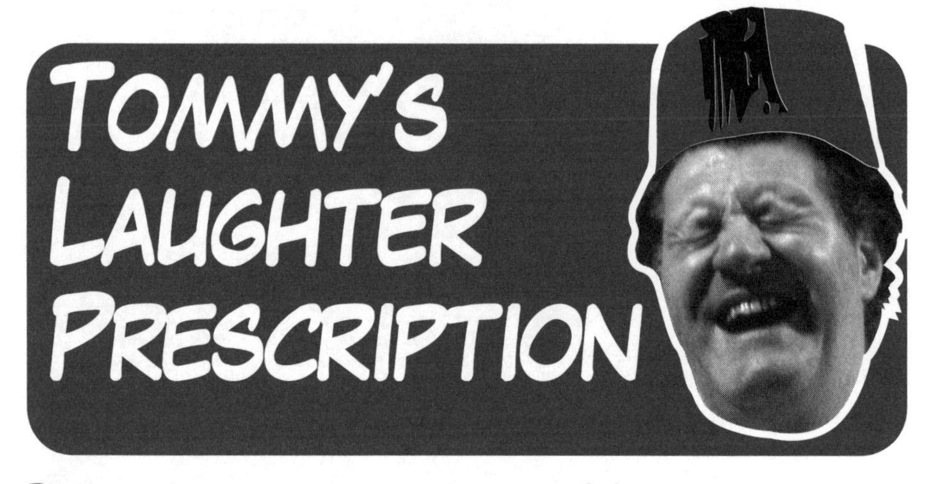

DOES MY VOICE SOUND A BIT HOARSE? IT DOES A BIT, DOESN'T IT? TODAY I LOST MY VOICE - AND THE ONE I'M USING NOW I BORROWED SPECIALLY FOR THE SHOW.

SERIOUSLY THOUGH I DID GO TO THE DOCTOR TODAY AND HE SAID, 'OPEN YOUR MOUTH' AND HE SAID, 'A LITTLE RAW' - JUST LIKE THAT - SO I WENT 'GRRRR...' NOT LOUD. JUST 'GRRRR...' (SOFTLY)

AND HE SAID TO ME, 'WHILE YOU'RE HERE I'LL TEST YOUR EARS, BECAUSE WHEN YOUR VOICE GOES IT AFFECTS THE HEARING.' I SAID, 'RIGHT' AND HE SAID, 'WHAT I'M GOING TO DO IS THIS. I WANT YOU TO GO OVER THERE, AND I'LL GO OVER HERE, AND WHAT I'M GOING TO DO, I'M GOING TO WHISPER SOMETHING TO YOU AND I WANT YOU TO REPEAT IT.' I SAID, 'RIGHT.' SO HE WENT OVER THERE AND I WENT OVER THERE AND HE SAID, 'HOW NOW, BROWN COW?' SO I SAID, 'HOW NOW, BROWN COW?' HE SAID, 'PARDON?'

SO I SAID TO THE DOCTOR, 'HOW DO I STAND?'
HE SAID, 'THAT'S WHAT PUZZLES ME.'

I SAID, 'DOCTOR, I FEEL LIKE A PAIR OF CURTAINS.'
HE SAID, 'THEN PULL YOURSELF TOGETHER.'

'DOCTOR, DOCTOR,' I SAID, 'THERE'S SOMETHING WRONG WITH MY FOOT. WHAT SHOULD I DO?' HE SAID, 'LIMP.'

THE DOCTOR SAID, 'YOU'RE IN SHOCKING SHAPE. DO YOU DRINK HEAVILY?' I SAID, 'NO, BUT I'M WILLING TO LEARN.'

I SAID, 'CAN YOU GIVE ME SOMETHING FOR MY LIVER?'
HE GAVE ME A POUND OF ONIONS.

I THOUGHT I HAD INDIGESTION. THE DOCTOR SAID, 'WHAT HAVE YOU BEEN EATING?' I SAID, 'OYSTERS.' THE DOCTOR SAID, 'HOW DID THEY LOOK WHEN YOU OPENED THEM?'
I SAID, 'DO YOU HAVE TO OPEN THEM?'

THE DOCTOR ASKED ME IF I TOOK MY TEMPERATURE.
I SAID, 'NO. IS IT MISSING?'

I SAID, 'DOCTOR, CAN YOU GIVE ME SOME SLEEPING PILLS FOR MY WIFE.' HE SAID, 'WHY?' I SAID, 'SHE WOKE UP!'

I SAID 'DOCTOR, I GET THESE TERRIBLE DREAMS.'
HE SAID, 'WHAT'S THAT?' AND I SAID, 'I KEEP DREAMING THESE BEAUTIFUL GIRLS, THESE BEAUTIFUL GIRLS KEEP COMING TOWARDS ME, KEEP COMING TOWARDS ME - I KEEP PUSHING THEM AWAY - THESE BEAUTIFUL GIRLS KEEP COMING TOWARDS ME AND I KEEP PUSHING THEM AWAY, PUSHING THEM AWAY.' HE SAID, 'WHAT DO YOU WANT ME TO DO?' I SAID, 'BREAK MY ARM!'

Sunday Show

1/. Pillow in bed, laying this side & the other side. Wife rolled her hair gag. Door Bolted Gag.

2/. Doctor, I'm losing all sense of direction – what shall I do? Get lost.

3/. Old Lady across the street gag. into Ploughman's Lunch.

4/. Finish now with a song:- "When you walk through the storm keep your head up high" – I did that & I fell in a puddle!

5/. Irishman looking in mirror gag.

I SAID, 'DOCTOR, I'M LOSING ALL SENSE OF DIRECTION. WHAT SHOULD I DO?' HE SAID, 'GET LOST.'

Tommy at the Seaside

You know, I was in Margate last summer for the summer season. A friend of mine said you want to go to Margate – it's good for rheumatism. So I went and I got it. And I tried to get into a hotel – it was so packed. So I went to this big boarding house and I knocked at the door and the landlady put her head out of the window and said, 'What do you want?' I said, 'I wanna stay here.' She said, 'Well stay there,' and she shut the window. And while I was there I bought one of these skin diving outfits. Have you seen them? Like a frogman's suit. Bought the whole thing – goggles, flippers, tank on the back. And I had a photograph taken like that – and like that! You never know, do you? You never know. And I went to the pier and I jumped in, cos you're not supposed to dive in – it's dangerous. And I jumped in like that and I think I turned a little bit on the way down and I went down about a hundred and fifty feet. It was lovely – very quiet – and I'm going along like that. *(Makes swimming gesture with right arm, holding left hand out in front of him)* I've got the instructions here! And I get rid of them and start going out like that *(Mimes with other arm)* and the feet are going like that *(Makes flipper movement with hands)* – not in the front, in the back – do you know what I mean? And I don't care now. I'm all over the place – the goggles getting all misty – and I'm humming to myself – not loud – just zzzzzz *(Very low)* and all of a sudden I saw a man walking towards me in a sports jacket and grey flannels. I thought that's unusual for a Tuesday. So I went towards him – moving like this – and I got right up to him and I got this pad out and wrote on it, 'What are you doing down here walking about in a sports jacket and grey flannels?' And he took this pad from me and wrote on it, 'I'm drowning.'

TOMMY AND HIS DOG

I was dog-tired last night – I slept in a kennel!

I've got a dog, you know.
I have. He's a one-man dog. He only bites me.

He took a chunk out of my leg the other day.
A friend of mine said, 'Have you put anything on it?'
I said, 'No, he liked it as it is.'

I'm only joking. He's harmless, really. But he's getting on a bit.
I said to him, 'Attack,' and he had one.

I just bought a watchdog and what do you think he watches? TV!

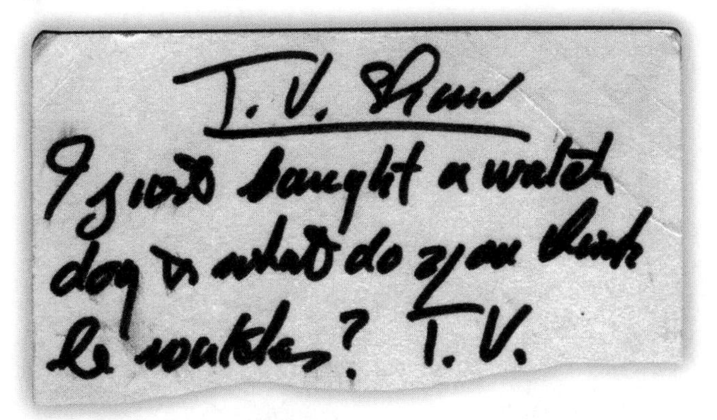
T. V. Show
I just bought a watch dog & what do you think he watches? T. V.

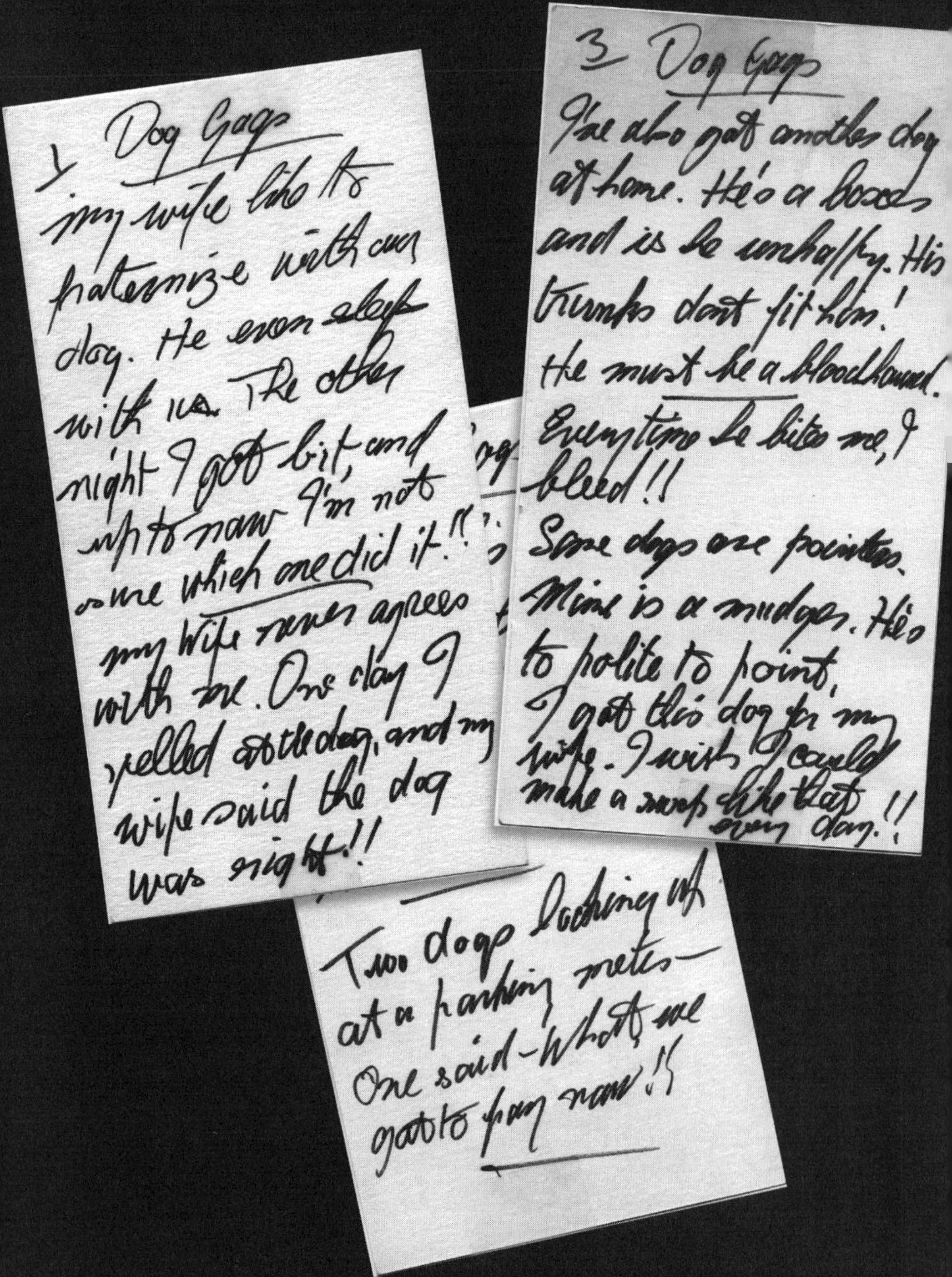

1 Dog Gags

my wife likes to fraternize with our dog. He even sleeps with us. The other night I got bit, and up to now I'm not sure which one did it!!

my wife never agrees with me. One day I yelled at the dog, and my wife said the dog was right!!

3 Dog Gags

I've also got another dog at home. He's a boxer and is he unhappy. His trunks don't fit him!

He must be a bloodhound. Everytime he bites me, I bleed!!

Some dogs are pointers. Mine is a nudger. He's to polite to point.

I got this dog for my wife. I wish I could make a swap like that every day!!

Two dogs looking up at a parking meter—

One said—What, we got to pay now!!

My wife likes to fraternise with our dog. He even sleeps with us. The other night I got bit and up to now I'm not sure which one did it!

My wife never agrees with me. One day I yelled at the dog and my wife said the dog was right!

I've also got another dog at home. He's a boxer and is he unhappy! His trunks don't fit him.

He must be a bloodhound. Every time he bites me, I bleed!!

Some dogs are pointers. Mine is a nudger. He's too polite to point.

I got this dog for my wife. I wish I could make a swap like that every day!

Two dogs looking up at a parking meter – one said, 'What! We've got to pay now?'

I had a dog that was so silly he chased parked cars!!

I bought my girl a lapdog, but she got rid of it. Every time she sat on the dog's lap it bit her!

COOPER'S LAUGHTER ALLSORTS

THIS FELLOW KNOCKED AT A DOOR AND SAID, 'HELLO. IS CHARLIE IN?' THE WOMAN REPLIED, 'CHARLIE DIED LAST NIGHT.' THE MAN SAID, 'HE DIDN'T SAY ANYTHING ABOUT A POT OF PAINT, DID HE?'

HERE'S A QUICK JOKE. THERE'S A MAN, SEE, AND HE'S SITTING ON TOP OF A BUS AND HE'S GOT A BANANA STICKING OUT OF HIS EAR. A BANANA STICKING OUT OF HIS EAR! WELL, ANOTHER MAN SAW THIS, COS HE WAS WATCHING HIM LIKE THAT. AND HE SAID TO HIMSELF, 'WELL, I MUST TELL HIM.' WELL HE WOULD, WOULDN'T HE? SO HE WENT UP TO HIM AND HE SAID, 'EXCUSE ME.' AND THE MAN SAID, 'SPEAK UP. I'VE GOT A BANANA STICKING OUT OF MY EAR!'

WHAT A WONDERFUL DAY IT'S BEEN. DO YOU KNOW IT'S BEEN SEVENTY DEGREES IN THE SHADE. I WAS CLEVER. I STAYED IN THE SUN! ACTUALLY, I DID A LITTLE BIT OF SUNBATHING. I WAS LYING OUT THERE TODAY. A LITTLE BOY CREPT ACROSS AND POURED SOMETHING ALL OVER MY BACK. HE SAID, 'THIS'LL MAKE YOU BROWN.' I SAID, 'WHAT IS IT?' HE SAID, 'GRAVY!'

DID YOU HEAR THE JOKE - THERE WAS A FOREMAN ON A BUILDING SITE AND HE LOOKED TO THE MAN AT THE TOP OF THE LADDER AND HE SAID, 'YOU - GET YOUR MONEY AND YOUR CARDS. YOU'RE FINISHED.' HE SAID, 'EH?' HE SAID, 'GET YOUR MONEY AND YOUR CARDS. YOU'RE FINISHED.' HE SAID, 'EH?' HE SAID, 'FORGET IT. I'LL SACK SOMEBODY ELSE!'

TROOPER COOPER

Tommy joined the Guards several weeks before the outbreak of the Second World War, serving latterly in North Africa and eventually joining the Combined Services Entertainment Unit in the Middle East until his demob in 1947.

Isn't it funny? Even in the army everything went wrong with me. It did really. I shall never forget when I first joined. They said to me, 'Would you like a commission?' I said, 'No – just a straight salary!'

There's this about the army – you never have to decide on what to wear. I just tried on my old army uniform and the only thing that fits is the tie.

There's this about the Army – you never have to decide on what to wear. I just tried on my old Army uniform and the only thing that fits is the tie.

When I was in the army my uniform fitted me like a glove. It covered my hand!

We had a sergeant and he used to call us out for roll call, you know, at four o'clock in the morning. Pitch black it was and he had a huge hurricane lamp in his hand and he used to say, 'Good morning, men' and we used to say, 'Good morning, lamp.' We couldn't see him!

And when you're on guard duty, they always teach you when you hear someone coming towards you in the dark to say with the rifle, 'Halt – who goes there – friend or foe?' You had to do that! 'Halt – who goes there – friend or foe?' *(Mimes drill)* Like that. And if they say 'Friend', you say 'Pass, friend.' Right. And I was on guard. I was on guard duty and it was very dark and I heard footsteps. 'Halt! Who goes there? Friend or foe?' And a voice said, 'Foe.' I said, 'How tall are you?' He said, 'Nine foot six.' I said, 'Pass, foe!'

I was seven years in the Horse Guards. It's like only yesterday. Now there's this sentry on guard duty and it's about four o'clock in the morning. It's very dark and he's got the rifle there *(Mimes accordingly)* and he's marching up and down and he's standing there about four o'clock in the morning and he falls asleep. Now that's a crime. I mean, they could put you inside for that straight away. So he's standing there asleep like that – he's standing there and all of a sudden the sergeant comes round the corner with the orderly officer. And now he's standing right in front of him. And there he is asleep *(Tommy looks dozy)* and there's the sergeant major like that *(Tommy looks fierce)*. And all of a sudden the sentry opens his eyes just a little bit like that – not much – just a little bit, and he can see them standing there. So he's gotta think now, hasn't he? He has, or otherwise he's gonna be inside. So he waits for a second and he's standing there and he opens his eyes like that and he says, 'Amen!' Huh, huh. It's lucky I wasn't court-martialled!

Cooper's Fez Tales

Everybody asks me where it came from. I'll tell you. I was in Egypt. In the army. Used to wear a pith helmet in the act in those days. A pith helmet, can you imagine? Not quite the same is it? Anyhow, one day I lost the bloody thing. Had to grab the first hat I could find. Then this waiter came by wearing one of these. That was that.

Then a few years ago I went back to Egypt with the wife. There was this guy selling fezzes in the market. I went to try one on and he turned to me and said, *'Just like that.'* I said, 'How do you know that? That's my catchphrase.' He said, 'Catchphrase? I know nothing about any catchphrase. All I know is that every time an English person tries one on, they turn to their friends and say, *"Just like that!"*' And then he said, 'You're the first one not to say it.' Priceless, isn't it?

Tommy in the Jungle

Now, here's a quick joke. What was it? Oh yes!

Did you hear the story of the king of the jungle? You know – the king of the jungle – the lion. And one day he woke up – he had a very bad temper – and he said to himself, 'I've just got to go outside now and teach them all who's the king of the jungle. Just to teach them.' So he gets up and he goes, 'Ooaarrhh!!' He was really mad. You know what I mean. 'Ooaarrhh!' And he saw a little chimp and he said, 'You! Who's the king of the jungle?' and he said, 'You, you're the king of the jungle.' 'Well that's alright then – alright.' And he walked along a bit more and he came across a laughing hyena and he said, 'Hey you, laughing boy.' And he went 'Hah hah hah hah hah! Hah hah hah hah hah!' He said, 'Who's the king of the jungle?' 'Ooh, hah hah hah! You are, you are.' So he walked on a little bit further and right at the very end was an elephant and a gorilla talking. And this gorilla looked at the elephant and he said, 'Here he comes, Jumbo. He's gonna do that king of the jungle bit again. He always does it.' He said, 'I'm not gonna stand it any more. I'm gonna leave you.' And he went up a tree. He said, 'I'll give you a trunk call later!' Hah hah hah! So the lion went up to this elephant and he said, 'Hey you!' He said, 'I'm talking to you big ears.' He said, 'Who's the king of the jungle?' And this elephant got his trunk and wrapped it right round him and threw him up in the air and as he was up in the air coming down he was going, 'Who's the king of the jungle? Who's the king of the jungle?' And he hit the ground hard and the elephant picked him up again and he threw him against the tree and he threw him against the other one. Then the other one and the other one! And the lion sank to the ground like that. It may have been like that. No, it was like that! And he said to the elephant, 'Look, there's no good getting mad just because you don't know the answer!'

HOMAGE TO MAX MILLER

The pre-eminent stand-up comedian of his era, Max Miller was the inspiration for a whole new generation of British comedians, not least Tommy Cooper. His sparkling personality and brilliant technique rightly earned him the label of 'The Pure Gold of the Music Hall.'

I've got the best wife in England. The other one's in Africa. 'Ere!
The other day I came home and the wife was crying her eyes out.
I said, 'What are you crying for?' She said, 'I'm homesick.' I said, 'This is your home.' She said, 'I know. I'm sick of it!'

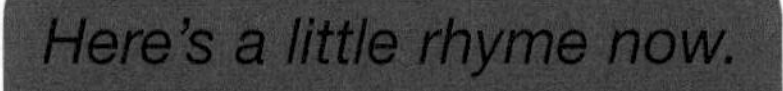

Adam and Eve
in the garden dwelt,
They were so happy
and jolly.
I wonder how they
would have felt
If all the leaves
had been holly!

(TOMMY PICKS UP ON INDIVIDUAL LAUGH OF WOMAN CACKLING IN THE CROWD)

I KNEW YOU WERE IN, BUT DIDN'T KNOW WHERE YOU WERE SITTING!

SO I SAID TO THIS LADY, I SAID, 'ARE YOU FAMILIAR WITH SHAKESPEARE?' SHE SAID, 'AS A MATTER OF FACT I AM. I HAD DINNER WITH HIM LAST NIGHT.' I SAID, 'WHAT ARE YOU TALKING ABOUT? HE'S BEEN DEAD FOR YEARS.' SHE SAID, 'I THOUGHT HE WAS QUIET.' 'ERE!

THERE'S A LADY OVER THERE GOT OPERA GLASSES ON ME. SHE THINKS I'M A RACEHORSE!

My wife came in the other day and she said, 'What's different about me?' And I said, 'I don't know - what is different about you? Have you had your hair done?' She said, 'No.' I said, 'Have you got a new dress on?' She said, 'No.' I said, 'Have you got a new pair of shoes?' She said, 'No.' I said. 'Well what is it? What's different?' She said, 'I'm wearing a gas mask.'

There's a man won the football pools, see, and he said to himself, 'I'll buy a car.' So he went down to the salesroom and saw the salesman and he said, 'I'd like a car. How much is that?' He said, 'Eight hundred pounds.' He said, 'I can't afford that. Eight hundred pounds? I only won seventy-five pounds.' 'Well,' the salesman said, 'How about a bicycle?' He said, 'I don't want a bike. I want to get out in the country to get some fresh air.' 'Well,' he said, 'how about a pair of skates?' He said, 'Get away! I want to get out. I don't want skates.' And the man said, 'I tell you what. How about a hoop and a stick?' He said, 'Alright.' So he bought a hoop and a stick and he went out into the country, came across a pub, and put the hoop and stick in the car park. He went inside, had a drink, came out and the stick's gone. Somebody's pinched it. So he went back to the landlord and said, 'Somebody's taken my stick. They've pinched it.' And the landlord said, 'Don't get excited. It can't have cost you much.' He said, 'Well, it only cost me half a crown, but that's not the point. How am I going to get home?'

MEET THE WIFE

Although her real name was Gwen, Tommy always referred to his wife as 'Dove.' They met while they were both performing for the troops soon after the Second World War and married in Nicosia on 24 February 1947. The marriage endured until the day he died.

HER BROTHER SAID TO ME, 'SHE SMOKES IN BED,'
AND I SAID, 'WHAT'S THE MATTER WITH THAT?
LOTS OF PEOPLE SMOKE IN BED.'
AND HE SAID 'WHAT, FACE DOWN?'

IN
Her brother said to me, "She smokes in bed," and
I said "Whats the matter with that, lots of people
smoke in bed," and he said "what? Face down."
X

She said to me, "Do you mind if I wear my hair
in a bun," I said, I don't care if you wear it in
a loaf of bread."
X

SHE SAID TO ME, 'DO YOU MIND IF I WEAR MY HAIR
IN A BUN?'
I SAID, 'I DON'T CARE IF YOU WEAR YOUR HAIR IN A
LOAF OF BREAD.'

AND SHE'S ALWAYS ON A DIET, MY WIFE. ALWAYS ON A
DIET. SHE'S ON A DIET NOW. EATS NOTHING BUT COCONUTS
AND BANANAS ALL DAY LONG. COCONUTS AND BANANAS.
SHE HASN'T LOST ANY WEIGHT, BUT YOU SHOULD SEE HER
CLIMB TREES!

MY WIFE - SHE'S ALWAYS ON A DIET. SHE'S ON ONE NOW.
SHE DRINKS EIGHT GLASSES OF WATER A DAY.
SHE'S LOST EIGHT POUNDS AND GAINED FIFTY GALLONS.

MY WIFE WANTED HER FACE LIFTED. THEY COULDN'T DO IT,
SO FOR TWENTY POUNDS THEY LOWERED HER BODY.

THE WIFE. IT'S HER BIRTHDAY NEXT WEEK AND I NEVER KNOW WHAT TO GET HER. I DON'T KNOW WHETHER TO GET HER A BOX OF CHOCOLATES, A DIAMOND RING, A FUR COAT OR NEW CAR.
THAT'S WHAT I'LL GET HER - A BOX OF CHOCOLATES!

IN ACTUAL FACT MY WIFE JUST PHONED ME BEFORE THE SHOW.
SHE SAID, 'I'VE GOT WATER IN THE CARBURETTOR.'
I SAID, 'WHERE'S THE CAR?'
SHE SAID, 'IN THE RIVER.'

MY WIFE HAS STOOD BY MY SIDE EVER SINCE WE WERE MARRIED - BUT THEN WE HAVE ONLY ONE CHAIR IN THE HOUSE. OH DEAR!

MY WIFE USED TO SAY, 'I'D GO TO HELL AND BACK FOR YOU.'
I SAID, 'YOU DON'T HAVE TO COME BACK JUST FOR ME.'

MY WIFE SAID, 'YOU'LL DRIVE ME TO MY GRAVE.'
I HAD THE CAR OUT IN TEN MINUTES.

I'VE JUST GIVEN THE WIFE A JAGUAR. I HOPE IT TEARS HER TO PIECES.

SHE WAS LOOKING AT A WOMAN'S MAGAZINE AND SHE SAW THIS FUR COAT.
SHE SAID, 'I WANT THAT.' SO I CUT IT OUT AND GAVE IT TO HER.

I GOT A NEW CAR FOR THE WIFE YESTERDAY - NOT A BAD SWAP!

THAT FACE OF HERS! WHEN SHE SUCKS A LEMON, THE LEMON PULLS A FACE.

SHE SAID, 'THE STOVE HAS GONE OUT.' I SAID, 'LIGHT IT.' SHE SAID, 'I CAN'T. IT'S GONE OUT THROUGH THE CEILING.'

SHE UNDERCOOKS EVERYTHING. WE HAD OXTAIL SOUP THE OTHER NIGHT AND THE TAIL WAS STILL WAGGING!

WHEN SHE COOKS YOU GET A LUMP IN YOUR THROAT - IN YOUR STOMACH - YOUR ARMS - YOUR LEGS.

ALL SHE WANTED TO DO WAS EAT OUT. SO WE ATE OUT IN THE GARAGE!

MY WIFE WAS IN THE BEAUTY SHOP TWO HOURS. THAT WAS JUST FOR THE ESTIMATE!

DO YOU WANT TO DRIVE YOUR WIFE CRAZY? WHEN YOU GO TO BED, DON'T TALK IN YOUR SLEEP. JUST GRIN.

I LIKE THE WAY SHE HOLDS HER HEAD - UNDER HER ARM!

My wife was in the beauty shop two hours. That was just for the estimate!!
Do you want to drive your wife crazy? When you go to bed don't talk in your sleep.
Just grin!!

I DID HER PORTRAIT IN OILS.
SHE HAS A FACE LIKE A SARDINE!

I FOUND A WAY TO CURE MY WIFE OF FALLING OUT OF BED.
I MAKE HER SLEEP ON THE FLOOR.

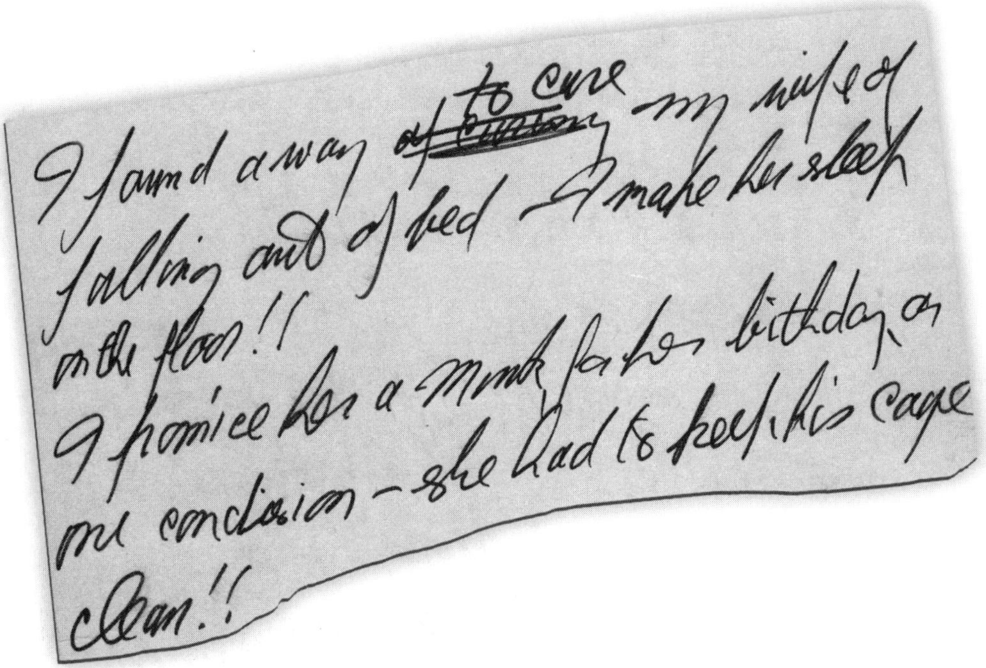

I PROMISED HER A MINK FOR HER BIRTHDAY ON ONE CONDITION - SHE HAD TO KEEP HIS CAGE CLEAN!

A LORRY CAME ALONG AND KNOCKED HER DOWN AND I SAID TO THE DRIVER, 'WHAT'S THE MATTER WITH YOU? WHY DIDN'T YOU GO ROUND HER?'
HE SAID, 'I DIDN'T HAVE ENOUGH PETROL.'

SHE WORE HER MOTHER'S WEDDING DRESS.
IT WAS A BIT TIGHT - HER MOTHER WAS STILL IN IT!

Tommy Dreams

You know I've been getting these terrible bad dreams. Terrible. The other night I dreamt I was eating a ten-pound marshmallow. When I woke up the pillow had gone!

Last night I dreamt I was plucking a chicken. Woke up the next morning and the wife was bald.

Some people sleep in pyjama trousers, and some people sleep in pyjama tops. Me? I just sleep in the string!

I slept like a baby last night
– with my foot in my mouth.

I slept like a baby last night – with my foot in my mouth!

These days you cant trust anybody – last
night I walked in my sleep and when I got
back someone walked off with my mattress.

These days you can't trust anybody. Last night I walked in my sleep and when I got back someone had walked off with my mattress.

Boy, am I tired! I was up half the night trying to remember something I wanted to do. Then it dawned on me – I planned to go to bed early!

If you've got insomnia, don't lose any sleep over it!

They've got a new cure for insomnia – a pill that weighs 200 pounds. You don't swallow it – you drop it on your head.

They gave me a lovely dressing room – all made of tile with 14 taps!!
If you've got insomnia – don't lose any sleep over it!
They've got a new cure for insomnia, a pill that weighs 200lbs. You don't swallow it, you drop it on your head!!
He was so bow legged his wife hung him over the door for good luck!

I couldn't sleep last night so I got up at three a.m. and made tea in my pyjamas. I couldn't find the teapot anywhere!

I couldn't sleep last night got up 3AM, & made tea in my pyjamas I couldn't find the tea pot anywhere!! —

I feel good tonight. I was up at the crack of six this morning. Took a brisk walk to the bathroom and was back in bed at five past six.

TOMMY'S ONE-LINERS

Did you see me pick that up? I'm not afraid of work!

I went to a plastic surgeon – he looked almost real.

I missed my catnap today – I slept right through it.

I played golf the other day – got a hole in one – the other sock was perfect.

I feel good tonight. There's nothing like a cold bath – full of hot water!

I've got acting in my blood – many years ago a straight actor bit me!

I'm so near-sighted I can't even see my contact lenses.

I was just thinking – what do you give to a sick florist?

She was bowlegged, he was knock-kneed – when they stood together they spelled OX!

Have you ever been to an Eskimo wedding? They blow out the cake and eat the candles.

I went in a pub and had a ploughman's lunch – he wasn't half mad!

I've tiptoed into my house so often at 4 a.m. in the morning, my neighbours think I'm a ballet dancer.

I went golfing the other day. I dug up so many worms, I decided to go fishing!

Now here's a quick laugh. Do this tomorrow. Go into an antique shop and say 'What's new?'

They always say take an aspirin for a headache – who wants a headache?

Did you hear the joke about the fire eater? She hiccupped and cremated herself?

Did you hear about the Salvation Army drummer who quit because his mother didn't want him hanging around on street corners!

Did you hear about the Salvation Army drummer who quit because his mother didn't want him hanging around on street corners!

I was a dancer once. I was. I did Swan Lake. I fell in.

I said 'I'd like a cornet, please.' She said, 'Hundreds and thousands?' I said 'No. One will do me very nicely.'

TOMMY ON STAGE

Here's a little trick for you now.
In fact it's a matter of life and death.
I shall now attempt to throw these three cards into that hat there, so I'd like a drum roll please.
(Stands back at a distance and scales first card in direction of the hat...)
Missed! *(Repeats with second card...)*
Missed!
Now if I miss this time, I'm going to shoot myself. *(Repeats with third card and misses again...)*
Missed!
(Goes to table, picks up gun in exasperation, goes into wings, a gunshot is heard, then after the briefest of pauses Tommy walks back...)
Missed!
Huh huh huh!

Phone in piano – Rings: Voice –
Is dat T. C. T. Yes. – V. Well I like
to ask you something. T. Not now. I'm
in a middle of a show:- Voice:- What show
are you watching?..!! T. You must be nuts.'
Voice:- You think I'm nuts – who ever
heard of anyone keeping a phone inside
a piano.!!

(Half-way through his act the phone rings in the piano – Tommy picks up the receiver)

Voice: Is that Tommy Cooper?

Tommy: Yes.

Voice: Well, I'd like to ask you something.

Tommy: Not now – I'm in the middle of a show.

Voice: What show are you watching?

Tommy: You must be nuts.

Voice: You think I'm nuts! Whoever heard of anyone keeping a phone inside a piano.

And now, ladies and gentlemen, this trick I'm gonna show you now is pretty dangerous. I could break my neck doing this ...

(Tommy takes off his jacket and draws attention to two chairs balanced precariously on a small table which has been brought on stage by two stagehands...)

...so, if I meet with an accident, I'd like to take my applause now.

(Tommy beckons audience to applaud...)

I'm not gonna break my neck for that!

(Tommy puts jacket back on, dismisses stagehands, who remove the furniture, and nothing more is said of the matter!)

TOMMY AND HIS AGENT

Tommy's love-hate relationship with his agent and manager became legendary in show business circles. In the thirties Miff Ferrie had himself been famous as the leader of the Jackdauz, a popular music combination of the day.

I've got a clause in my contract that says I have to be cremated – so that my agent can get ten per cent of my ashes!

He's only dull and uninteresting until you get to know him. After that he stinks!

He's only dull and uninteresting until you get to know him. After that he stinks!!

He's so crooked he has to screw ~~his socks~~ on his socks!!

If he offer you a deal see a lawyer. And if the lawyer approves, see another lawyer!!!

He's so crooked he has to screw on his socks!

If he offers you a deal, see a lawyer. And if the lawyer approves, see a second lawyer.

Success never changed him. He's still the same arrogant swine he was when he was a failure!

He said, 'Here's a cheque for your trouble.' I said, 'I haven't had any trouble.' He said, 'Wait until you cash that cheque!'

TOMMY GOES DOWN MEMORY LANE

Some of the places I played in the early days! I was doing the act at this club one night. They were throwing bread rolls at me and trying to knock my fez off and I was scared out of my mind – these were the hard men of London out there – and I didn't know what to do, so I just said, 'Stop that!' I don't know what possessed me. But I had to say something. The place came over funny. 'Stop what?' shouted this geezer. I said, 'Why, stop throwing all these bread rolls and that.' 'And why should I stop?' he shouted back. 'Well, because I haven't got an ad-lib for people throwing bread rolls at me.' The place fell about. It was never quite so hard after that, but you're never completely home and dry.

Cooper's Heckler Stoppers

One does not readily associate this type of audience-combative humour with Cooper, but these lines, dating from the early part of his career, show that he was anxious to be prepared for all eventualities.

Heckler – Stoppers

The last time I saw a head like that a jockey was bending over it

If anyone puts a price on your head — take it.

He can't match wits with me — I haven't got any wits to match him with.

Its just lucky for you that I'm a scholar, a gentleman and a coward.

How would you like to come out to my car and smell the exhaust pipe?

"Good for you. You made a joke. What are you trying to do — top your parents?")

The last time I saw a head like that a jockey was bending over it.

If anyone puts a price on your head – take it.

He can't match wits with me – I haven't got any wits to match him with.

It's just lucky for you that I'm a scholar, a gentleman and a coward.

How would you like to come out to my car and smell the exhaust pipe?

Good for you – you made a joke. What are you trying to do – top your parents?

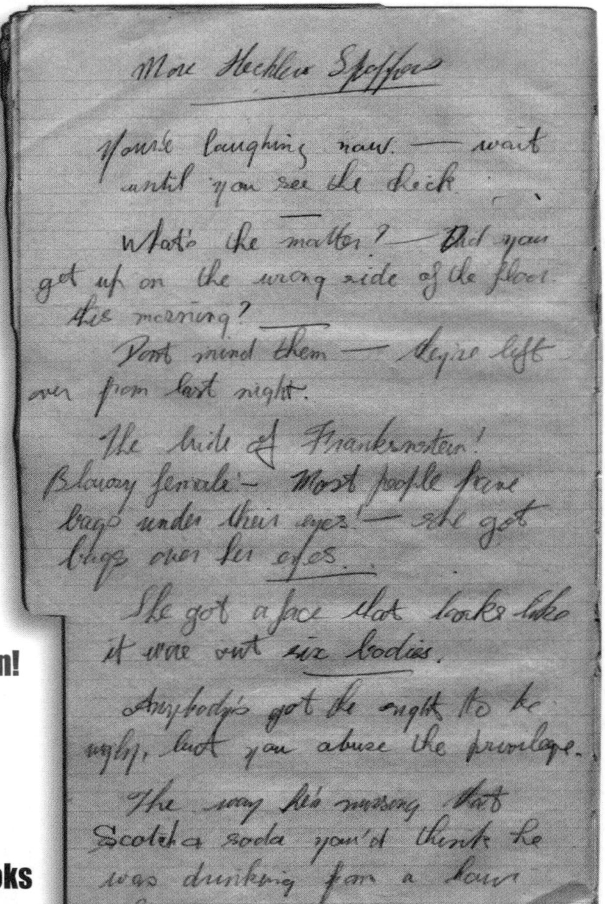

You're laughing now – wait until you see the cheque.

What's the matter – did you get up on the wrong side of the floor this morning?

Don't mind them – they're left over from last night.

(Of a blousy female) The bride of Frankenstein! Most people have bags under their eyes! She's got bags over her eyes.

She's got a face that looks like it wore out six bodies.

Anybody's got the right to be ugly, but you abuse the privilege.

The way he's nursing that scotch and soda, you'd think he was drinking from an hour glass.

I never forget a face, but in your case I'll make an exception.

His head is so big, he can't get a headache to fit him.

TOMMY'S EARLY STAND-UP

OPENING OF SHOW
Excuse me Sir, — Have you
seen a tall good-looking
man in Evening Dress, wearing
a Fez. — I'm lost!!!
Just call me Razor Blade
— I'm sharp tonight! Do you
know the funniest thing
happen to me comming to
the Studio tonight. (LAUGH)
— I wish I could remember
what it was. It's not funny
but it takes up time. ~~Well~~ By the way
how do you like my new
suit — do you think
the style will ever come back

Excuse me, sir. Have you seen a tall good-looking man in evening dress wearing a fez – I'm lost!!! Just call me razor blade – I'm sharp tonight!

Do you know the funniest thing happened to me coming here tonight. I wish I could remember what it was. It's not funny, but it takes up time.

By the way, how do you like my new suit? Do you think the style will ever come back?

POST CARD
ADDRESS TO BE WRITTEN ON THIS SIDE

Fits well. —
This is not my
stomach — I've
just got a low chest!!
I was told it was
a special show
tonight. — So I'm
wearing my tails
"PRODUCE TAILS"
INTO — Card Trick
A GAG → Handkerchief Trick
Chinese Ping Pong
Stop thinking for a
minute EXIT.
EXTRA. RABBIT FLAT.

Fits well. This is not my stomach – I've just got a low chest!

I was told it was a special show tonight – so I'm wearing tails.

(Tommy reaches down and produces a couple of actual fox tails)

Please! Please! The other acts'll think it's a fix – and they'd be right.

You're such a lovely audience – you deserve me!

What a reception! Who did the warm-up? Bob Hope?

Everybody's saying television is here to stay. I don't know. The Hire Purchase company is taking mine back tomorrow.

I was at a show last week. They said money was no object, so they didn't give me any.

I've been ill. Yes, I was in bed with 104 – and let me tell you, that's a lot of people in one bed.

Please relax. Just treat me as the interval.

I'm sorry I'm a bit late, but I had to pour water over my smoking jacket.

I've been waiting so long I forgot my act.

I've been lying low for months – my bed sags. I'm not myself. What can you expect of a day that begins with getting up?

Two psychiatrists pass each other on the street. One says, 'Hello.' The other says, 'I wonder what he meant by that.'

Keep it up. Flattery will get you somewhere. I started here six months ago and it seems only yesterday, and you know what a lousy day yesterday was.

COOPER'S PUB TALES

I WAS OUT IN THE PUB HAVING A DRINK JUST BEFORE THE SHOW AND I WAS STANDING THERE AND I FELT A HAND GOING INTO MY POCKET. A HAND. SO I LOOKED ROUND AND I SAW THIS MAN STANDING THERE WITH HIS HAND AND I SAID, 'WHAT ARE YOU DOING?' HE SAID, 'I'M LOOKING FOR A MATCH.' I SAID, 'WHY DIDN'T YOU ASK ME?' HE SAID, 'I DON'T TALK TO STRANGERS.'

I WENT ON A DRINKING MAN'S DIET. YOU JUST DRINK AND DRINK AND DRINK UNTIL YOU FALL OVER. HOW DO YOU LOSE WEIGHT? TRYING TO GET UP!

A BIG WHITE HORSE WALKS INTO A PUB. THE BARMAN SAID, 'WE HAVE A DRINK NAMED AFTER YOU.'
THE HORSE SAID, 'WHAT? ERIC?'

A TRAMP WALKED INTO A PUB AND YELLED, 'WHAT'S THE MATTER WITH EVERYBODY? NOBODY'S GOT WHAT I WANT!' 'WHAT DO YOU WANT?' ASKED THE BARMAN AND THE TRAMP SAID, 'CREDIT!'

A DRUNK DROVE HIS CAR ALL THE WAY DOWN FROM MANCHESTER TO LONDON. THE POLICE ASKED HIM WHY HE DROVE DOWN IN THAT CONDITION. HE SAID, 'THEY WOULDN'T LET ME ON THE PLANE LIKE THIS!'

A DRUNK STAGGERED OUT OF A PUB AND JUST MADE IT TO THE PARKING METER. HE PUT A SIXPENCE IN THE METER AND HUNG ON FOR DEAR LIFE, WHEN A POLICEMAN WALKED OVER AND SAID, 'COME ON - GET GOING - MOVE ALONG.' AND THE DRUNK SAID, 'NOT YET. I'VE STILL GOT TWENTY MINUTES LEFT!'

COOPER CLASSIC 1

Now, do you know – I was cleaning out the attic the other day – with the wife – filthy, dirty, and covered with cobwebs – but she's good to the kids. And I found...

(Tommy goes behind table and reaches down to bring out...)

... this old violin and this oil painting. So I took them to an expert and he said to me, 'What you've got there – you've got a Stradivarius and a Rembrandt. Unfortunately...

(Tommy's eyes survey the audience with a mixture of disappointment and suspicion, as only his could)

...Stradivarius was a terrible painter and Rembrandt made rotten violins!'

(At which point Tommy pushes the violin through the canvas and slings them both aside)

Tommy's Lucky Dip

DO YOU KNOW I HAD A FUNNY DREAM LAST NIGHT? I DREAMT I WAS A CANNON AND I SHOT OUT OF BED AND WHEN I GOT UP I REALISED I WAS WALKING FUNNY AND I SAID TO MYSELF, 'THAT'S FUNNY.' I DID. I SAID, 'THAT'S FUNNY.' AND I WENT TO THE DOCTOR ABOUT IT AND I SAID, 'I'M WALKING FUNNY.' HE SAID, 'IF YOU DON'T MIND ME SAYING SO, YOU'VE GOT ONE LEG SHORTER THAN THE OTHER.' I SAID, 'I DO MIND YOU SAYING SO.' OH, I DID! I WAS FIRM. I WAS FIRM. I SAID, 'I DO MIND YOU SAYING SO.' I SAID, 'I THINK YOU'VE GOT A DOWNRIGHT CHEEK.' HE SAID, 'NO, YOU'VE GOT A DOWN RIGHT CHEEK. THAT'S WHY YOU'RE WALKING FUNNY!'

THERE WAS MOTHER BEAR, FATHER BEAR AND BABY BEAR AND THE BABY BEAR SAID, 'WHO'S BEEN EATING MY PORRIDGE?' AND THE FATHER BEAR SAID, 'WHO'S BEEN EATING MY PORRIDGE?' AND THE MOTHER BEAR SAID, 'WHAT'S ALL THE TROUBLE? I HAVEN'T MADE IT YET.'

HERE'S A QUICK JOKE - I MUST TELL YOU THIS - I WANT TO HEAR IT MYSELF! IT'S ABOUT THE FAITH HEALER AND HE SAID TO THIS MAN, 'HOW'S YOUR BROTHER?' AND HE SAID, 'HE'S ILL.' AND THE FAITH HEALER SAID, 'NO, NO, NO. HE ONLY THINKS HE'S ILL.' HE SAID, 'NO, HE'S ILL - HE LOOKS ILL - HE LOOKS ILL.' HE SAID, 'NO.' HE SAID, 'I'M TELLING YOU. HE LOOKS ILL - I LOOKED AT HIM THE OTHER DAY - HE LOOKS ILL.' SO THREE WEEKS LATER HE MET HIM AGAIN. HE SAID, 'HOW'S YOUR BROTHER?' HE SAID, 'HE THINKS HE'S DEAD.'

Musical Cooper

I have an electric guitar that doesn't need electricity. It burns coal!!

The other day I bought a piano stool and I've taken it back six times. I turn it in every direction and I still can't get a single note out of it.

I broke my arm and I went to the doctor. And I said, 'Doctor when it's mended will I be able to play the piano?' and he said, 'Of course you will,' and I said, 'That's funny. I couldn't play before.'

This conductor was giving his
orchestra a stiff rehearsal - when
he dropped his baton. He said
'Trombone player was playing his
instrument too loud.' 'Trombone
player hasn't got here yet'
'Alright - when he gets here tell
him he was playing too loud.'

This conductor was giving his orchestra a stiff rehearsal when he dropped his baton. He said, 'The trombone player was playing his instrument too loud.' Someone said, 'The trombone player hasn't got here yet.'
He said, 'Alright, when he gets here tell him he was playing too loud.'

I'm very musical. A lot of people don't know this, but I was born with a banjo on my knee – the doctors had to operate before I could get my trousers on.

This man said, 'What does your father do?' I said, 'He was a conductor.'
He said, 'Musical or on the buses?' I said, 'Neither. He was struck by lightning!'

PHILOSOPHICAL COOPER

Did you know, I read the other day that twenty per cent of driving accidents are caused by drunken drivers? That must mean then that the other eighty per cent are caused by drivers who are stone cold sober. In other words, if all drivers got drunk, there would be far less accidents.

If you drink and drive, remember alcohol and petrol don't mix – well, they do, but the taste's terrible!

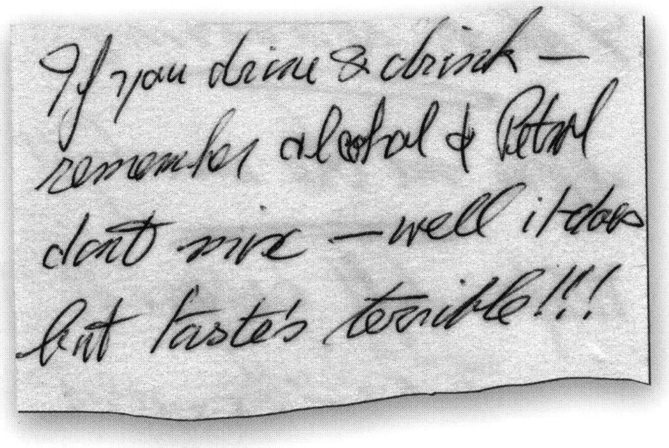

Remember when you drive, don't drink – you may spill it!

It's like garages, isn't it? Wherever they put a petrol pump they find petrol!

Maybe I should copyright myself – people impersonating me all the time. I mean it's not the principle – it's the money!

My father was a great philosopher and he said to me, 'It doesn't matter if you let love slip through your fingers or even money slip through your fingers, but if you let your fingers slip through your fingers you're in trouble.' That's semi-jolly, isn't it?

Let a smile be your umbrella and you'll get soaking wet.

The only good thing about rain is that you don't have to shovel it!

Why do the people you hate most have the best luck?

How do the birds know when you've just cleaned your car?

A waiter is a man who believes that money grows on trays.

Somebody once said that horsepower was a very good thing when only horses had it.

Does a cat wash his face – or does he wash his feet and wipe them on his face?

If you're feeling low, eat a box of Lux – you're bound to bubble over!

Do you know what's embarrassing? When you look through a keyhole and see another eye!

Show me a man with two feet on the ground and I'll show you a man who can't take off his trousers.

A lady has a baby every five minutes. We've got to find her and put a stop to it.

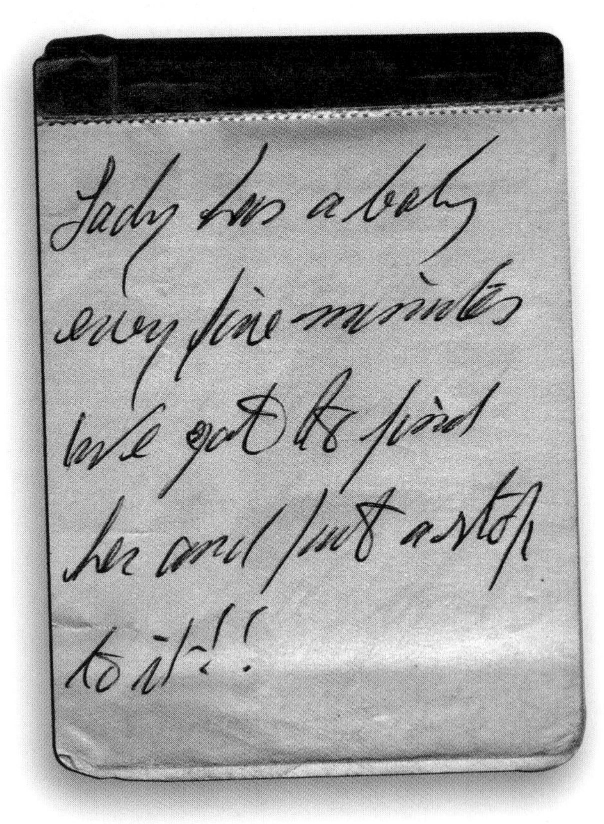

Lady has a baby
every five minutes
we've got to find
her and put a stop
to it!!

M is for the million things she gave me…
O means that she's only growing old…
T is for the tears she shed to save me…
H is for her heart so pure of gold…
Put them altogether…
They spell **MOTH**!

The ballet is something I can't understand. All those girls dancing around on their toes. I figure if they want taller girls – why don't they get 'em?

There were six chorus girls. Five married millionaires and one of them married a poor man. And do you know something? She's the only one who's miserable!!

I always say a friend in need is a pest – get rid of him. And if at first you don't succeed, forget it!

T.C.

I'd like to leave you with these words – One good turn – gets most of the blankets.

I'd like to leave you with these words – one good turn gets most of the blankets.

MEET THE FAMILY

My boy came towards me the other day with his arms out and he walked slowly towards me. He went 'Dad, dad, dad.' Oh – it was wonderful – he's only fifteen. He'll be sixteen soon, if I let him. Oh dear!

My boy complains about headaches
– I told him a thousand times. –
when you get out of bed its feet
first!!

My boy complains about headaches. I told him a thousand times – when you get out of bed it's feet first!

The other day he had an accident. He went into a barber shop for a haircut and came out with the wrong head!

My daughter is always washing her face. I know that cleanliness is next to godliness, but after she gets through washing her face she irons it!

This mother had eleven children. Her kids got so noisy, so she told them, 'The first one in this house who screams is going to get a mouth full of soap.' And do you know, I can still taste the stuff!

There were eleven of us in our family and we were so poor we used to wear each others' clothes. I didn't mind, but I had ten sisters.

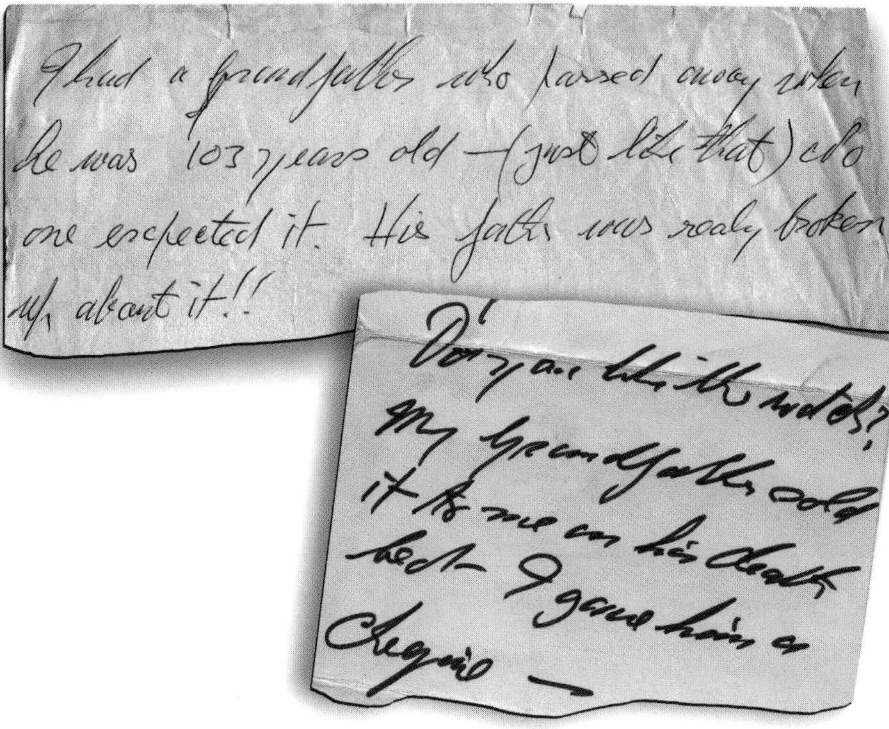
I had a grandfather who passed away when he was 103 years old – (just like that) No one expected it. His father was really broken up about it!!

Do you like the watch? My grandfather sold it to me on his death bed – I gave him a cheque –

I had a grandfather who passed away when he was 137 years old – *just like that!* No one expected it. His father was really broken up about it!

Do you like my watch? My grandfather sold it to me on his death bed – I gave him a cheque!

I've been looking up my family tree. They were all enjoying their bananas!

My little boy said to me today, he said, 'What do you call a gorilla that's got a banana in each ear?' And I said, 'What do you call a gorilla that's got a banana in each ear?' He said, 'Anything you like – he can't hear you!'

Tommy at the Dentist

Oh, my teeth itch!

A dentist had to pull a horse's tooth, which he found easy, but the tough part was getting the horse to sit in the chair!

I always wanted to be a dentist, but my hands were too big. Before I could get to the back teeth, I had to pull out all the front teeth.

I went to the dentist. He said my teeth are all right, but my gums have got to come out. He looked at me and I said, 'I've got a terrible pain just up there – see. *(Shows by putting finger in his mouth)* Up there it was. And he said, 'I tell you what I'll do' and I said, 'What's that?' Cos he spoke to me and I said, 'I've got a pain up there.' He said, 'I tell you what I'll do – I'll X-ray it.' So he got these tiny X-rays like that – little small ones like that and he put it up there like that. He put it up there like that. And I'm sitting there like that and he brings this X-ray machine in – see there – and it went *(Makes drilling sound)* like that and he took it out and he looked at it and he said, 'No wonder it hurts – you've got a finger poked up there!'

Cooper à la Carte

YOU KNOW, I HAD A MEAL LAST NIGHT. I ORDERED EVERYTHING IN FRENCH. I SURPRISED EVERYBODY. IT WAS A CHINESE RESTAURANT.

AND I SAID TO THIS WAITER, I SAID, 'THIS CHICKEN I'VE GOT HERE'S COLD.' HE SAID, 'IT SHOULD BE. IT'S BEEN DEAD TWO WEEKS.' I SAID, 'NOT ONLY THAT,' I SAID, 'IT'S GOT ONE LEG SHORTER THAN THE OTHER.' HE SAID, 'WHAT D'YOU WANT TO DO? EAT IT OR DANCE WITH IT!'

I SAID, 'FORGET THE CHICKEN.' I SAID, 'GIVE ME A LOBSTER.' SO HE BROUGHT THE LOBSTER. I LOOKED AT IT. I SAID, 'JUST A MINUTE,' I SAID, 'IT'S ONLY GOT ONE CLAW.' HE SAID, 'IT'S BEEN IN A FIGHT.' I SAID, 'WELL, GET ME THE WINNER!'

I SAID, 'HAVE YOU GOT FROG'S LEGS?' HE SAID, 'YES.' I SAID, 'WELL, HOP OVER THE COUNTER AND GET ME A CHEESE SANDWICH!'

AND I SAID TO THIS CHINESE WAITER, I SAID, 'TELL ME SOMETHING.' I SAID, 'ARE THERE ANY CHINESE JEWS?' HE SAID, 'I DUNNO. I'LL GO AND FIND OUT.' SO HE WENT AND HE CAME BACK. HE SAID, 'NO. THERE'S ONLY APPLE JUICE, PINEAPPLE JUICE, AND ORANGE JUICE.' THANK YOU!

I SAID, 'WAITER, WHAT'S THAT IN MY SOUP?' HE SAID, 'I'D BETTER CALL THE BOSS, BECAUSE I CAN'T TELL ONE INSECT FROM ANOTHER.'

A GIRL BEHIND THE BAR SAID, 'WHAT WOULD YOU LIKE TO DRINK?' I SAID, 'I'LL HAVE A GIN... AND BITTER LEMON.' SHE SAID, 'HERE'S YOUR GIN AND WHAT DID YOU BITE MY LEMON FOR?'

You know it's not my day! I backed a horse today 20 to 1 – it came in 20 past 4. He was so late coming in he had to tiptoe back to the stables. And the jockey kept hitting him like that with a whip – like that – not like that – like that and the horse said, 'What are you doing that for? There's nobody behind us!'

I bought a greyhound about a month ago. A friend of mine said, 'What are you gonna do with it?' I said, 'I'm gonna race it.' He said, 'By the look of it, I think you'll beat it.'

You know my memory's terrible. I cut myself shaving today and I forgot to bleed.

My back's terrible. I was playing piggyback with my little boy. I fell off!

I get dizzy when I lick an airmail stamp!

I'm superstitious – I won't work a week with a Friday in it!

It's not my night. I've always been unlucky. I had a rocking horse once and it died.

I've got a cigarette lighter that won't go out.

I don't feel so good tonight. In fact, just before the show I met my life insurance agent and he took his calendar back.

I feel terrible tonight. Last night – one bottle of beer and I was out like a light. Someone hit me over the head with it!

I fell off the ironing board – I was pressing my trousers – and I forgot to take them off!!

I fell off the ironing board – I was pressing my trousers and I forgot to take them off!!

My wife and I used to go to race meetings and I was told to cut off a lock of her hair, for luck, for every race. Eventually we had a hundred thousand pounds in the bank and not a hair on her head.

I was there at Woolwich last week – the ferry was about ten feet from the quay. It could have been eleven feet. I think it was eleven feet. So I took a flying leap, cos I've got long legs, and I landed right on it and said to the man, 'I've just made it.' He said, 'You had plenty of time. I was coming in.'

I woke up and I felt awful, I really did. I thought I'd passed away and nobody had told me. And I started to read the paper – like you do – and I looked down the obituary column. I did. I read the whole list and when I saw my name wasn't there, I got up.

STATING THE OBVIOUS

'I FEEL A LITTLE LIGHT-HEADED!'

Tommy walks on stage carrying a portable oil stove…
Thank you very much. They just told me. They said, 'Go out there and warm them up.' Huh huh huh!

This fellow said to me yesterday, 'Do you always drink your gin neat?' I said, 'No. As a matter of fact, sometimes I don't wear a tie and have my shirt hanging out.'

Do you know I've had a pain here all day?
(He reaches inside his jacket and brings out a small square of glass)
Look at that – oh dear!
(He tosses it aside and picks up a golf club)

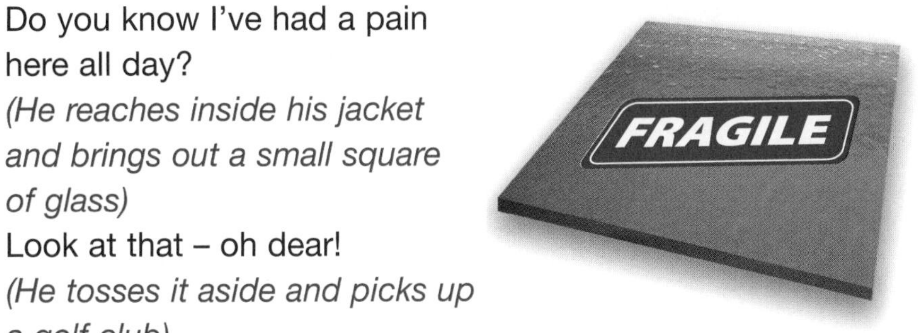

I joined a golf club last week.
(He separates club into two pieces)
It keeps coming apart!

(He places a piece of tissue paper in a metal dish and applies match …whoosh!)
Just a flash in the pan!

Oh, my feet are killing me – you know every night when I'm lying in bed they get me right round the throat like that!

And now a tap dance!
(He picks up string with tap tied on the end and jiggles it about – then picks up glove...)
See that glove...
(He releases another glove, sewn to first glove at the fingertips)

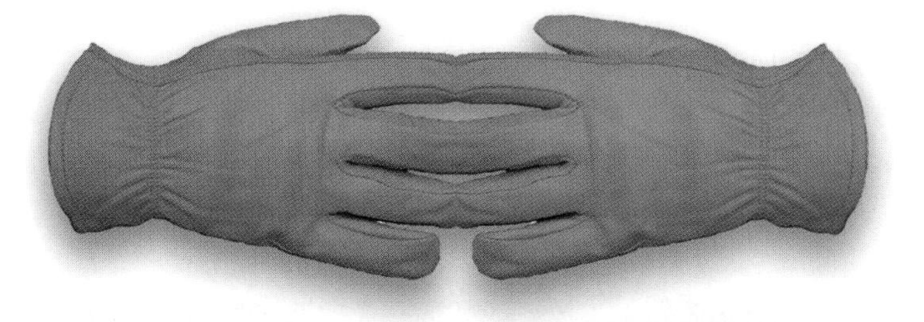

Look, second hand!

(He picks up a skipping rope, looks at it...)
Here we have a skipping rope – so we'll skip that!
(...and throws it away...)

Now, before we go any further, I'd just like to say this. It's a funny word, this. I mean, how many times could you go on stage and this will get a laugh? This, it's a funny word that. Now that, that's funnier than this...

Look, see that *(Tommy holds up left hand and wriggles its fingers)*

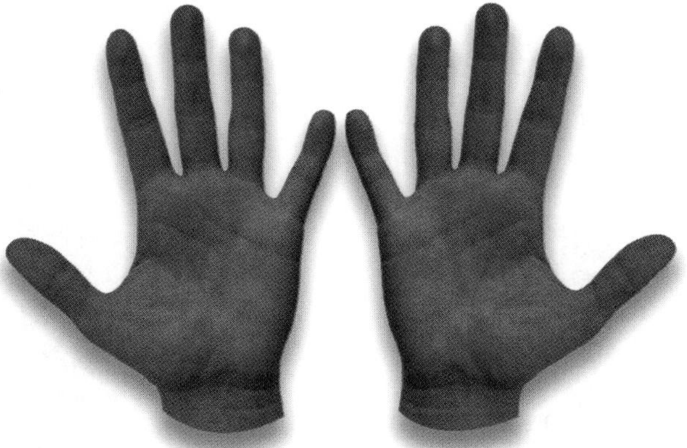

– well this one's just the same! *(Repeats with other hand)*

(He puts on a pair of joke spectacles with horns attached) Look! Horn-rimmed glasses! I should be locked up!

Do you know what the bald-headed man said when he received a comb for Christmas? 'I'll never part with it!'

(A stagehand now walks across carrying one half of a life-size, head-to-toe cardboard cut-out of Tommy…)
That's my half-brother!

I'd like now to show you a photograph of that wonderful escapologist, Houdini.
(He picks up an envelope, takes out a piece of blank card, shows it...

...and slings it to one side)
He's got away again!

One of the studio staff said, 'Tommy, do you like bathing beauties?' I said, 'I don't know. I've never bathed any!'

(Tommy picks up a small Viking horn and gives it a single toot...)
It doesn't sound much, does it?
But in five minutes from now this place will be full of Vikings.

(He picks up a light bulb...)
Light bulb!

(...and drops it on an old-fashioned pair of scales)
Heavy bulb!

(Then a pack of cards, which he proceeds to play like a mouth organ)

Playing cards!

When some women feel the urge to love, they get married. I know a girl who wanted someone to love, so she bought a German shepherd. Not a dog, a real German shepherd!

(He picks up a stick of pink peppermint seaside rock...)
I will now turn this stick of rock into furniture.
(He breaks it into three pieces...)
One – two – three!

(...and tosses the three pieces over his shoulder)
Three-piece suite! Eh?

Two cannibals were eating a clown – one said to the other, 'Does he taste funny to you?'

Now to finish I'd just like to sing you one little song – 'When you walk through the storm, with your head held high' – I did and I fell in a river!

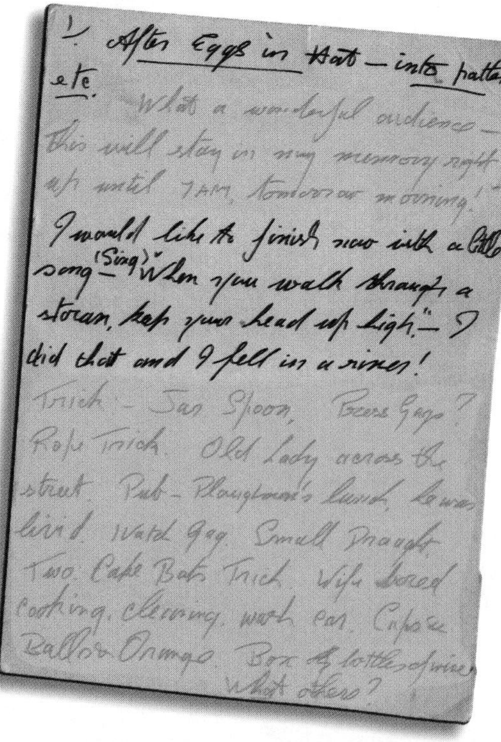

Tommy the Boxer

This routine from Tommy's early career reflects his love of the sport. He always said that the best thing about his time serving in the Guards was the boxing, at which he excelled. His height and bulk made him a natural.

I used to be a boxer, but I had to give it up. I couldn't learn to pick up my teeth with gloves on!

I come from a long line of boxers – except my father – he was a Dalmatian!

I'm still in good shape. I can still go ten rounds – as long as someone is buying them!

I used to be a boxer. They used to call me Canvasback Cooper. I did pretty good at the beginning. I won my first ten fights, then I ran into trouble. They made me fight a man! I used to go into the ring vertical and come out horizontal. My best punch was a rabbit punch, but they wouldn't let me fight rabbits.

Boxing 2

What a fight! when the bell rang, I came out of my corner and threw six straight punches in a row. Then the other fellow came out of his corner. First he threw a right cross, then he threw a left cross. Then came the Red Cross. He came up to about my chin. The trouble was he came up too often.

What a fight! When the bell rang, I came out of my corner and threw six straight punches in a row. Then the other fellow came out of his corner. First he threw a right cross, then he threw a left cross. Then came the Red Cross. He came up to about my chin. The trouble was he came up too often.

In the fifth round I had my opponent worried. He thought he killed me. But in the sixth round I had him covered with blood – mine! I had so much resin on my back that whenever I passed the Albert Hall, the fiddlers used to stand at attention. Then I brought one up from the floor – which is where I happened to be at the time.

Boxing 3

In the fifth round I had my opponent worried. He thought he killed me. But in the sixth round I had him covered with blood – mine!! I had so much resin on my back that whenever I passed Albert Hall, the fiddles used to stand at attention. Then I brought one up from the floor – which is where I happened to be at the time.

After that fight they gave me a cup – to keep my teeth in. Just before the fight started, my manager yelled in my ear that my opponent beat his wife, kicked his children and starved his mother. That made me really fighting mad. If there's one thing I can't stand, it's someone yelling in my ear!

I wasn't taking any chances. In my right glove I had a horseshoe, a bag of cement and an anvil. Only one thing kept me from winning that fight. I couldn't get my glove off the floor! First I gave him my left. Then I gave him my right. After that I was through. I didn't have anything left for myself!

Cooper Classic 2

There was an Irishman, a Mexican and a German taken prisoner. I don't know where – they were just taken prisoner. And they were ordered to be flogged, see. So they said to the Mexican, 'You can have anything on your back, whatever you like to ease the pain.' So he said, 'I'll have olive oil.' So they rubbed it all over his back like that *(Tommy mimes the application of oil to the prisoner's back)* and they went, 'Crunch – crunch, crunch, crunch.' *(He mimes ferociously with imaginary whip)* 'And crunch!' I put that extra 'Crunch' in! And he flopped on the floor and they dragged him out. And it was the German's turn and he stood there like that. *(Tommy stands rigid to attention)* And they said, 'What do you want on your back?' He said, 'Nein.' That means 'Nothing,' doesn't it? So they got the whip and they went, 'Crunch, crunch – crunch, crunch, like that.' *(Tommy mimes, even more agitated than before)* He just stood there. He didn't bat an eyelid, didn't bat an eyelid. And it was the Irishman's turn and they said, 'What do you want on your back?' He said, 'I'll have the German!'

BACK WITH THE AUDIENCE

It's only natural to be nervous at the beginning of a show – but please don't be. I want you to enjoy yourselves this evening. There is no need to laugh or applaud. Just forget that I'm the sole support of a wife and a family. Forget that I'm pure at heart. Forget that I served the country for five desperate years in a lonely foxhole in the steaming jungles of Burma. Forget all that! If you don't want to laugh or applaud, I won't care!

Wouldn't it be funny if I looked up and you were all gone? I've had a request, but I'm not leaving until I'm good and ready.

They gave me a lovely dressing room – a nail. That's the first time I ever had a dressing room where I have to tip the attendant.

I wish I had a Polaroid camera so that I could get a close-up of that joke dying.

We've got a brilliant show for you tonight. Brilliant. The best ever. And if I'm telling you one word of a lie, may I be struck down on this very spot. *(Tommy moves away from the spot and looks upward…)*

What a wonderful audience – this will stay in my memory right up until seven a.m. tomorrow morning.

Thanks for coming in for my audition. Next week I'm going back in show business.

Now get ready for this one – it's one of the first jokes I ever stole.

When I'm not doing tricks, I put on a floor show – I demonstrate vacuum cleaners!

A little boy said to me, 'One reason I like watching your show is because as soon as it's over a better one comes on!'

Come back tomorrow night. I'll be opening in person.

At least you can try and laugh from memory.

I see we have a very reserved group here, so if I happen to say something funny just nod and I'll understand.

One more joke like that and my picture won't be in the lobby anymore – I'll be hanging out there in person.

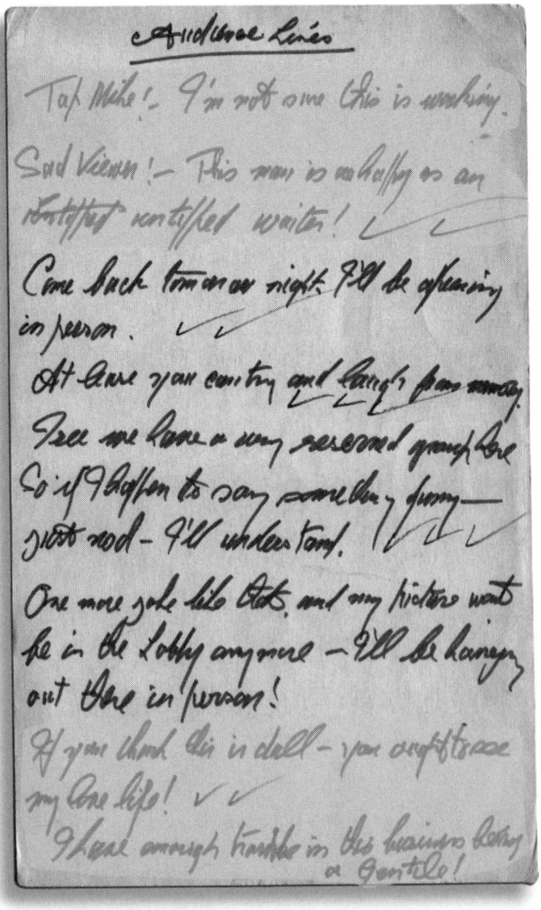

Cooper's Animal Crackers

Do you know, I was walking down the street the other day. I know a lot of people say that, but I was. And I saw this little fence so I looked over it and there was this little chicken, a little Rhode Island Red, and he must have been psychic because he looked up and went, 'Cluck, cluck.' So I went, 'Cluck, cluck' and then he went, 'Cluck, cluck.' So I went, 'Cluck, cluck.' And this policeman came along and he arrested us both for using foul language!

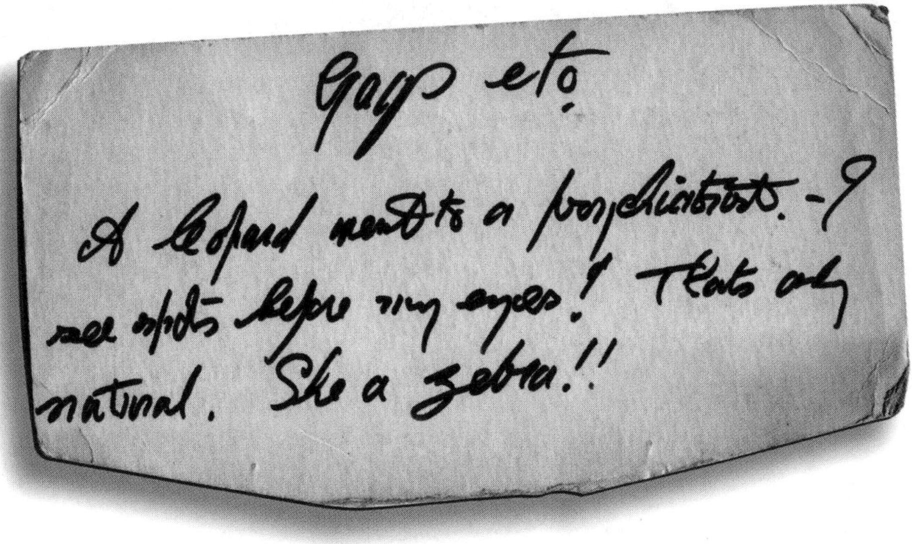

A leopard went to see a psychiatrist. He said, 'Every time I look at my wife I see spots before my eyes.' The psychiatrist said, 'That's only natural.' He said, 'But doctor, she's a zebra.'

Do you know that a grizzly bear crawls into a cave and sleeps for six months? Do you know why? Who's going to wake him up?

This elephant trod on a mouse. The giraffe said, 'Why did you do that?' He said, 'I didn't mean to. I only meant to trip him up.'

Elephants are remarkable animals. They travel for miles and miles over mountains and through the jungles to a place where they're going to die and they die there – the trip kills 'em!

There's a man having a barbecue in the front garden. So he's turning the spit like this and the flames are getting higher and higher – higher and higher, see – and he's singing. 'Oh sole mio… O sole mio, farewell.' And the flames are getting higher and higher and this drunk walks by and says, 'Your singing's alright, but your monkey's on fire!'

Farmer Brown had a parrot and he took him to town and he bought a crate of chickens. So he's coming back and he turns around and the parrot is sitting on the back – and all the chickens are walking. The parrot said, 'Look girls, when you listen to reason, you can ride!'

TOMMY AND THE LAW

I WAS ON MY WAY HOME FROM THE THEATRE THE OTHER NIGHT. I WAS WALKING HOME WITH THESE TWO SUITCASES, SEE, AND THIS POLICEMAN CAME UP TO ME AND IT'S AFTER MIDNIGHT AND THE POLICEMEN STOP YOU TO SEE WHAT YOU'VE GOT INSIDE. SO THIS POLICEMAN STOPPED ME, YOU SEE, AND HE SAID, 'WHAT HAVE YOU GOT IN THAT CASE THERE?' A BIT HARSH HE WAS. I SAID, 'WHAT HAVE I GOT IN THERE?' HE SAID, 'YES.' I SAID, 'IN THERE, I'VE GOT SUGAR FOR MY TEA!' HE SAID, 'AND WHAT HAVE YOU GOT IN THE OTHER ONE?' I SAID, 'IN THAT ONE I'VE GOT SUGAR FOR MY COFFEE.' AND THEN HE TOOK OUT HIS TRUNCHEON AND WENT 'BOOM'... (TOMMY MIMES STRIKING AND BEING DAZED AS A RESULT)...'THERE'S A LUMP FOR YOUR COCOA!'

I WAS WALKING HOME THE OTHER NIGHT. A MAN CAME OUT OF A DOORWAY. HE SAID, 'HAVE YOU SEEN A POLICEMAN AROUND HERE?' I SAID, 'NO.' HE SAID, 'STICK 'EM UP.'

DID YOU HEAR THE JOKE ABOUT THE POLICEMAN WHO STOPPED THIS MAN? HE SAID, 'RIGHT, GET OUT OF THE CAR. GET OUT.' HE SAID, 'I WANT YOU TO BLOW INTO THIS.' SO THE FELLOW WENT (TOMMY BLOWS) AND AS HE DID A BIG HORN CAME OUT OF HIS HEAD. SO HE SAID, 'DO IT AGAIN.' SO HE WENT (TOMMY BLOWS AGAIN) AND ANOTHER HORN CAME OUT. HE SAID, 'WHAT HAVE YOU BEEN DRINKING?' HE SAID, 'BOVRIL!'

DID YOU HEAR THE ONE ABOUT THE NEAR-SIGHTED BANK ROBBER. HE WENT INTO THE BANK. HE SAID, 'STICK EM UP.' *(TOMMY MIMES ACCORDINGLY)* 'ARE THEY UP?' HUH HUH HUH.

Man fell out of a tenth-story window. He's lying on the ground with a big crowd around him a policeman walks over and says — What happened? The man says, I don't know, I just got here!

A MAN FELL OUT OF A TEN-STOREY WINDOW. HE'S LYING ON THE GROUND WITH A BIG CROWD AROUND HIM. A POLICEMAN WALKS OVER AND SAYS, 'WHAT HAPPENED?' THE MAN SAYS, 'I DON'T KNOW. I JUST GOT HERE!'

THERE'S THIS FELLOW AND HE'S ROWING UP THE ROAD LIKE THAT. *(TOMMY MIMES ROWING ACTION)* NOT LIKE THAT, LIKE THAT! SO HE'S ROWING UP THE ROAD LIKE THAT, AND THIS POLICEMAN COMES UP TO HIM AND SAYS, 'WHAT ARE YOU DOING?' AND HE SAYS, 'I'M ROWING UP THE ROAD.' AND THE POLICEMAN SAYS, 'YOU HAVEN'T GOT A BOAT.' AND HE SAYS, 'OH, HAVE I NOT!' *(TOMMY MIMES AS IF SWIMMING FOR HIS LIFE!)*

MORE LAUGHTER ALLSORTS

Two guys were out in the passage talking. One said to the other, 'I hear we might be going out on strike – what are we striking for this time?' He said, 'Shorter hours.' The other replied, 'I'm in favour of that – I always thought sixty minutes was too long!'

There's a man in a country lane, and he's in snow up to here *(Tommy holds his hand at chest height)* – up to here like that see, and a man walks up to him and says, 'Dear, oh dear! Don't worry – I'll get a shovel and I'll get you out.' The man says, 'Get a big one – I'm sitting on a horse!'

A man walks down the street with a big red beard and two big horns coming out of his head. He knocks on a door and a woman answers. He says, 'I'm the Danish Bacon Viking. Do you eat Danish Bacon?' She said, 'No fear – if that's what it does for you!'

The taxi driver said, 'I'll take the kids for nothing.' The father turned to the kids and said, 'Okay – jump in, children, and have a nice ride. Your Mother and I will take the tube and see you there!'

There was this fellow. One day his wife said, 'Get out of bed and get a job.' His friend said, 'So what happened? Did you go out and get a job?' and he said, 'Are you kidding? Where can you find a job at five o'clock in the afternoon?'

TOMMY GOES ABROAD

Do you know I went to see my travel agent the other day, about my holidays, and I saw a picture of Majorca on the wall, and I said, 'I want to go there.' So he pinned me to the wall! But seriously, I went to Majorca and we went by plane – it's the only way to fly. And you know I always sit in the back, because you never hear of a plane backing into a mountain! It was the biggest thrill of my life when I stepped off that plane – it was still in the air! And I was looking out the window like that – it may have been like that! – no, it was like that – and I saw a man coming down in a parachute and he went like that to me. *(Tommy beckons with his fingers)* I said, 'I'm alright.' He said, 'Please yourself – I'm the pilot.' And it got a little bit rough in the air pockets like that and the plane was all over the place like that. *(He mimes with his arms outstretched)* And there was a little old lady sitting there in the plane and she got so nervous she started to pray and she looked at me and she said, 'Do something religious.' So I did. I took up a collection. And we're coming down to land fast – like that – fast – and it affects your ears, doesn't it? They go all funny, don't they? And the girl came in and gave me chewing gum. That's what they gave me – chewing gum – for the ears. Took me two days to get it out! And while I was there – in Majorca – I went into this bar, and all along the top of the bar were these bulls' heads, and right there in the middle there was this big bull's head. I mean the others were big, but this was really big. You know what I mean. And I said to the barman, 'That's a big bull.' And he said, 'I know, there's a sad story behind that bull.' And he looked like that *(Tommy does sad gesture)* and I said, 'Really?' and he said, 'That bull killed my brother.' I said, 'Really – was he a bull fighter?' He said, 'No. He walked in here one day and it fell on his head.'

Risqué Cooper

My uncle was 83 and wanted to marry a girl of nineteen. The doctor said, 'This could be fatal.' He said, 'If she dies, she dies!'

An agent said to a producer, 'I've got a girl who wears a size 102 bra!' The producer said, 'A 102 size brassiere? What does she do?' and the agent said, 'She tries to stand up.'

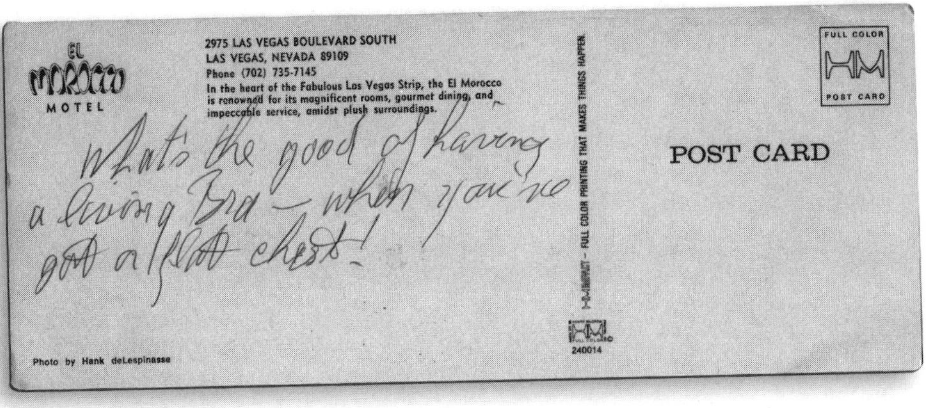

What's the good of a having a living bra when you've got a flat chest?

This man said to the policeman, 'This man started to hug me, kiss me, and embrace me!' The policeman said, 'Why didn't you run away?' He said, 'How could I in my high heels?'

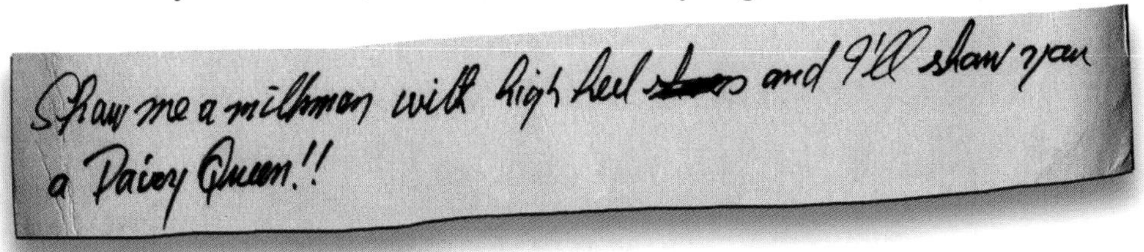

Show me a milkman with high heels and I'll show you a Dairy Queen!

Do you know the difference between bongo drums and sex? Well, you can't beat sex.

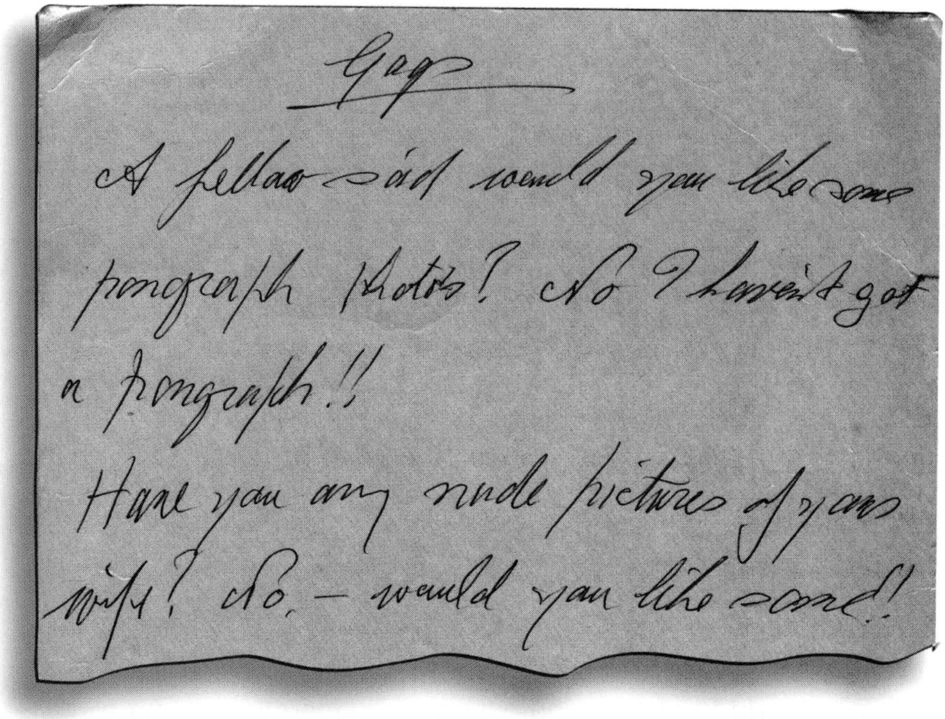
Gag

A fellow said would you like some pornograph photos? No I haven't got a pornograph!!

Have you any nude pictures of your wife? No. – would you like some!

A fellow said, 'Would you like some pornographic photos? I said, 'No, I haven't got a pornograph!!'

He said, 'Have you any nude pictures of your wife?' I said, 'No.' He said, 'Would you like some?'

I'm reading a book called 'Sex before 20.' Personally I don't like audiences.

If sex is a pain in the neck, you're doing it wrong.

If you think this is dull, you ought to see my love life.

My timing is off lately. When I sit down to eat I get sexy! When I go to bed I get hungry!

COOPER CLASSIC 3

Now there's something I wanna say.
There's a man went into a pub see and got a pint of beer. He drank the beer, put the glass on the counter, turned to the people on the right and said, 'You're a bunch of idiots' and he turned to the people on the left and he said, 'You're a bunch of fools' and he walked out. Next night he's back. Gets a pint, puts the glass on the counter and he turns to the right and he says, 'You're a bunch of idiots' and to the left, 'You're a bunch of fools' and he walks out. There was a man sitting there. And he said, 'Look, if he comes in tomorrow night – he may not come in – I don't know.' Well you don't know, do you? Well he may or he may not. Well you can't blame me, can you? I don't care. I don't know the fellow. I don't care if he comes in. Makes no difference to me. *(Tommy's voice gets more strangulated as he pleads)* But in he came. He came in, got the beer, drank the beer, put the glass on the counter, turned to the people. He said, 'You're a bunch of idiots and you're a bunch of fools.' And this man said, 'Just a minute. I'm not a fool.' He said, 'Well, join the idiots over there then.' Thank you.

MORE ONE-LINERS

I FEEL GOOD TONIGHT - I COULD CRUSH A GRAPE!

YOU KNOW, I JUST RECEIVED A LETTER FROM BILL BAILEY AND HE'S NOT COMING HOME!

I'M ON A WHISKEY DIET - LAST WEEK I LOST THREE DAYS.

I WENT TO AN OLD FILM YESTERDAY. BEN HUR. I LIKED BEN, COULDN'T STAND HER.

OH, I'VE GOT SOMETHING IN MY EYE. IT'S MY FINGER!

I FEEL SO NERVOUS TONIGHT, I MIGHT GET A TRICK RIGHT.

(ADDRESSED TO RUBBER CHICKEN) STOP HANGING ABOUT AND GET DRESSED!

I ALWAYS SAY DO UNTO OTHERS, BUT DO IT FAST.

THIS COULD DRIVE ME SANE.

ON THE OTHER HAND - I'VE GOT FOUR FINGERS AND A THUMB.

NOW THIS TRICK STARTS VERY SLOWLY AND GRADUALLY PETERS OUT.

BEFORE I GO I WOULD LIKE TO BE SERIOUS FOR A MOMENT. THAT'S ENOUGH!

MY LITTLE BOY LOVES THIS. I LOVE KIDS - I WENT TO SCHOOL WITH THEM.

COURTING COOPER

I'll never forget the first time we met. She was sitting on top of Waterloo Bridge – dangling her feet in the water. She cocked one eye at me and I cocked one eye at her and there we stood together cockeyed. And she had most unusual lips – both on top – and long blonde wavy hair – all down her back. None on her head – all down her back. And she had a very cute little button nose – I used to like the way it turned up, then down, then sideways – but I loved her and we had some wonderful happy times together. We used to go on the beach. She gave me a wave – I've still got it at home in a bucket. We used to go on the sands and play little games together. She used to bury me in the sand and then I buried her in the sand and one of these days I'm gonna go back and dig her up. And then she said she was hungry – so I bought her a stick of rock – and she bit it. And she went, 'Oh!' It wasn't quite so loud as that – it was more, 'Oh!' And then she started to cry a bit. I said, 'What's the matter, love?' She said, 'I've broken a tooth.' I said, 'Don't worry – you've got one left.' And when she stood up she had bow legs – she used to walk like that. I said to her, 'Why don't you learn to play the cello?' So I said to myself I'll take her to get some lovely teeth. So I got the best set of false teeth that money can buy. They looked beautiful – beautiful – and then after all that *(Tommy starts to cry)* – the money I spent on her – she left me – left me *(He's weeping buckets now).* And a year later I met her again and she came towards me and she just stood there and laughed at me – laughed at me – with my own teeth!

BACK AT THE DOCTOR'S

Oh dear – what a day I've had! I went to see my doctor. I had to – he's ill. He said, 'I want you to lie down on the couch.' I said, 'What for?' He said, 'I want to sweep up.'

I said, 'But seriously, doctor, I have broken my arm in several places.' He said, 'Well, you shouldn't go to those places.'

I said, 'It hurts me when I do this.' *(Tommy raises arm)* He said, 'Well, don't do it!'

And I said, 'Doctor, doctor, it hurts when I do this *(Tommy presses his elbow with his finger)*, and it hurts when I do this *(He presses his ear with his finger)*, and it hurts when I do this.' *(He presses his chest with his finger)* I said, 'What have I done?' He said, 'Broken your finger.'

Doctor:- You will live to be
seventy. P. says I am seventy
D. What did I tell you.

The doctor said to the patient, 'You will live to be seventy.' The patient said, 'I am seventy.' The doctor said, 'What did I tell you?'

My doctor goes to about six or seven hospitals a week. He's a very sick doctor.

Yesterday I went round to the doctor. There was nothing wrong with me – I just felt like sticking my tongue out at somebody.

What a doctor! For ten minutes he listened with a stethoscope – then he said, 'Just as I thought – dandruff!'

I've used saccharine for years and my doctor told me I had artificial diabetes!

Gags [illegible] in answer to absolutely no request.
I think I had better see a doctor
Every once in a while I blow smoke
rings. And I don't smoke!
I gave up smoking three years ago.
I went to a doctor and he said – whenever
you get the urge to smoke try a bar of
chocolate. I did but, I didn't like it!
I had trouble keeping them lit!!

I think I had better see a doctor. Every once in a while I blow smoke rings – and I don't smoke!

I gave up smoking three years ago. I went to my doctor and he said, 'Whenever you get the urge to smoke, try a bar of chocolate.' I did, but I didn't like it. I had trouble keeping them lit!

I read of a doctor whose prescriptions were so illegible that a patient used one for two years as a Railway Pass, got into theatres and football cup ties with it, and finally gave it to his daughter who played it on the piano and won a scholarship to the Royal College of Music!

Back in the Jungle

Now, here's a quick joke.

It was in the jungle see – in the jungle – and there was a hyena and he's talking to this monkey and he said, 'You see that little passage, that little narrow way down there – you see that big clump of trees and bushes,' and this monkey said, 'Yes.' And he said, 'Well, I go home that way every night. I don't have to, but you know it's a short cut for me and I go home' and he said, 'Every time I get to that bunch of trees there this lion jumps out and throws me all over the place.' He said, 'I don't know why he picks on me. Every time he keeps throwing me about and bashing me about and then he goes.' And he said, 'It's funny. D'you know what I mean?' So this monkey said, 'I know what you mean.' He said, 'I'll tell you what – I'll come over here tonight – you know – to protect you.' So the hyena said, 'Would you?' The monkey said, 'Yes.' So they shook hands on it – nothing in writing – and they started to walk down towards this clump of trees, see – huh, huh, huh – I can't help laughing. I know what's coming next! – and they got down to this clump of trees and he was just gonna turn like that and this lion turned and jumped out and got this hyena and went 'boom boom boom' and this monkey went right up the tree and left him there looking at him like that. And he was looking at him like that and all of a sudden this lion went 'boom boom' and left this hyena on his back like that – it may have been like that – no, it was like that – and then the monkey came down and was standing beside him and this hyena's like that and he looks up at this monkey and he said, 'What happened? I thought you were gonna help me.' He said, 'Well, I was, but when I looked down, you were laughing so much, I thought you were winning!'

THE MOST FAMOUS MAN IN BRITAIN

TALK ABOUT BEING RECOGNISED. I SHALL NEVER FORGET - I WAS GOING TO PLAY LEEDS, JUST OUTSIDE LEEDS, AND I WAS GOING UP BY PLANE. ANYWAY, IT GOT FOGGY AND WE WERE DIVERTED TO MANCHESTER. I WAS REALLY CROSS ABOUT IT, SO I GOT ALL MY PROPS AND CASES TOGETHER AND I THOUGHT I'LL GO AND HAVE A DRINK IN THE BAR. TRUE. AND I'M STANDING THERE AND NOT FEELING TOO HAPPY ABOUT IT AND A YOUNG FELLOW CAME UP TO ME AND SAID, 'HELLO. WHAT ARE YOU DOING HERE THEN?' NOW, THERE'S A LOT OF PEOPLE WALKING ABOUT, SEE, AND I SAID, 'WHAT AM I DOING HERE?' HE SAID, 'YES. WHAT ARE YOU DOING HERE?' AND I SAID, 'I TELL YOU WHAT,' I SAID, 'I'VE COME FROM LONDON, AND I LIVE IN CHISWICK, AND I GOT FED UP WITH WALKING AROUND THERE, SO I THOUGHT I'D COME UP HERE TO WALK AROUND HERE.' HE SAID, 'OH! HOW LONG YOU GONNA DO THAT FOR THEN?' AND I SAID, 'TILL I GET FED UP HERE, THEN I'LL GO BACK TO CHISWICK AND WALK AROUND THERE AGAIN!' THE PINHEAD!

YOU KNOW, A CHAP CAME OVER TO ME IN THE PUB THE OTHER DAY AND SAID, 'I SAW YOU IN CORONATION STREET LAST WEEK... GREAT!' 'SORRY,' I SAID, 'I WASN'T IN CORONATION STREET.' 'I'M SURE I SAW YOU IN CORONATION STREET,' HE INSISTED. I STILL SHOOK MY HEAD. THEN HE THOUGHT HARD FOR A WHILE, GRIPPED MY ARM AND SAID, 'NO, THAT'S RIGHT - SAW YOU IN SAINSBURY'S.'

ENCORE FOR MAXIE!

X. In the desert I met a Mummy—
I think she was looking for her
Daddy. She came right up to me and
said Fario, my Fario. I said I'm
not your Fario — She said, who are
you? I said, I'm
I came here for a
and pints. She
my eyes, what
I've got big eyes
looking all over
She looked into
for 2 thousand
for this moment
five. 2 thousand

She looked into my eyes and said
Wattell than gottell I gotta also
wattell than! I said how far
have you got to go — she said
half a league — and when I got there
I was in the second division — playing
for Chelsea — We started to walk
across the desert — five days and
five nights — we came to a tent — I
stood outside the tent — I wouldn't go in.
2 thousand years, old she was. We
stood outside the tent — she said
Thy people shall be my people
and my people shall be thy
people. And mind — no looked
[illegible] could have been anybody's

Yours Sincerely,
Max Miller.

I always have a wonderful time when I go on my holidays because I haven't got one of those wives who says, 'Where have you been? How much have you spent? Who have you been with?' She doesn't say that. She comes with me!

But she didn't come with me this time. I went to Africa, the north of Africa, and do you know the first thing I saw in the desert? A mummy. I think she was looking for her daddy! She came right up to me and said, 'Pharaoh, my Pharaoh.' I said, 'I'm not your Pharaoh.' She said, 'Who are you?' I said, 'I'm Mrs Cooper's son. I came here for a little bit of peace and quiet.' She kept on looking at my eyes. What was she after? My lashes? I've got big eyes. That's my mother's fault – looking all over England for my father! She looked into my eyes and said, 'For two thousand years I've waited for this moment. I am a blaze of fire.' I said, 'For two thousand years? You must be hungry. I'll get you some dates!' She looked into my eyes and said, 'Whither thou goest, I goest also whither thou.' I said, 'How far have you got to go?' She said, 'Half a league' and when we got there I was in the second division – playing for Chelsea! We started to walk across the desert – five days and five nights – then we came to a tent. I stood outside the tent. I wouldn't go in. Two thousand years old she was! We stood outside the tent. She said, 'Thy people shall be my people and my people shall be thy people.' And when we looked they could have been anybody's!

COOPER CLASSIC 4

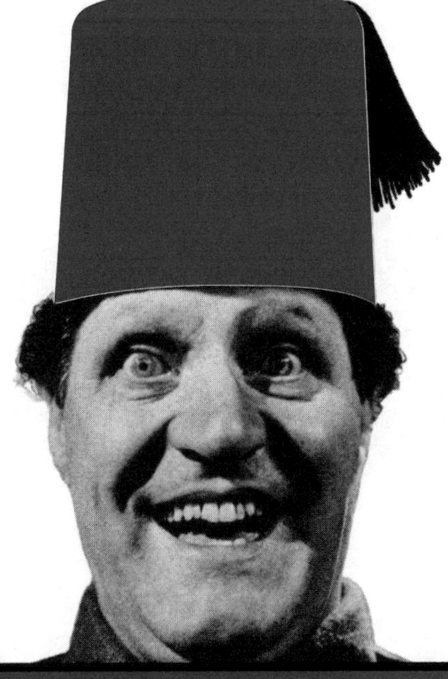

THERE WAS AN ENGLISHMAN, A SCOTSMAN AND AN IRISHMAN AND THEY WERE ARRESTED FOR BEING DRUNK IN THE STREET. SO THEY SAID - ONE OF THEM SAID - I'LL TELL YOU WHAT WE'LL DO - WE'LL GIVE ASSUMED NAMES.' THE OTHERS SAID (SLURRED), 'GOOD IDEA, YES.' SO THE POLICEMAN SAID TO THE ENGLISHMAN, 'WHAT'S YOUR NAME?' SO THE ENGLISHMAN LOOKED AROUND AT THE SHOPS AND SAW MARKS AND SPENCER, SO HE SAID, 'MARK SPENCER.' AND THE POLICEMAN SAID TO THE SCOTSMAN, 'WHAT'S YOUR NAME?' AND HE LOOKED AND HE SAW TIMOTHY WHITES, SO HE SAID, 'TIM WHITE.' AND HE SAID TO THE IRISHMAN, 'WHAT'S YOUR NAME?' AND HE LOOKED AND SAID, 'KENTUCKY FRIED CHICKEN.'

TOMMY GOES SHOPPING

Do you know, I went window shopping today. I bought four windows. And I went to the pet shop and said, 'I'd like to buy a wasp, please' and he said, 'We don't sell wasps.' So I said, 'Well, you've got one in the window.'

Then I went to buy some pork chops. I told the butcher to make them lean. He said, 'Which way?'

I went across to the barber shop. I said, 'How much is a hair cut?' He said, 'Twenty quid.' I said, 'How much is a shave?' He said, 'A fiver.' I said, 'Shave my head.'

The barber said to me, 'After you finish shaving, what do you want on your face?' I said, 'Leave the nose.' And he was slow. He was so slow. He looked at me. He said, 'Do you know your hair's turning grey?' I said, 'Well get a move on.'

I went into a chemist's and I said, 'Have you got anything for a headache?' He said, 'Yes.' So he gave me something and I paid him and he said, 'I toss you double or nothing.' So I lost. I walked out with two headaches!

These adverts are silly, aren't they? I saw one the other day. It said, 'Take this wonderful powder for a headache.' I mean, who wants a headache? And I went into a chemist's and I said to the man behind the counter – he was right down behind – I couldn't see him – I said, 'Excuse me, have you got anything for hiccoughs?' I said, *(Tommy raises his voice)* 'Excuse me' – I was a bit harsh – 'have you got anything for hiccoughs? *(At the top of his voice)* Have you got anything for hiccoughs?' And he jumped up and he hit me right across the face with a cloth. And I said, 'What did you do that for?' 'There you are,' he said, 'you haven't got hiccoughs now, have you?' I said, 'I never had them – it's for my wife out in the car.'

MEET THE WIFE AGAIN

T.V. Show

Evening! – Good welcome, and show to me evening! It's no good, I must rehearse everything!! into:– It's my bad memory – My wife also has a bad memory – she remembers everything!!! Top hat Riding gear, Gag. ("Two Head Gag Doctor)

My wife has a bad memory – she remembers everything!

The meals she cooks put colour in your face – purple!

I said to my wife, 'I can't eat this beef stew.' She said, 'Shut up! It's custard pie.'

I met my wife at a dance – I thought she was home with the kids. If she ever finds out she'll kill me.

One morning she ran after the dustman and said, 'Am I too late for the dustcart?' He said, 'No – jump in!!'

She puts on cream an inch thick – curlers in her hair – fishing net over the whole thing. She said, 'Kiss me.' I said, 'Take me to your leader!'

I remember the night I had a wreck in my car – now I'm sorry I married her.

She said, 'I've left the car in the dining room.' I said, 'How did you get the car in the dining room?' She said, 'It was easy. I made a left turn when I came out of the kitchen.'

Talk about driving – Once she left the garage at 50 miles an hour – Then she came back – She forgot the car!!

Talk about driving. Once she left the garage at fifty miles an hour. Then she came back. She forgot the car!

I took her to this restaurant and she said she wasn't hungry. So she asked for a side dish – a side of beef!

I asked the waiter, 'What can I get for my wife?' He said, 'I don't know. What are you asking for her?'

The doctor said my wife and I needed plenty of exercise – so I bought myself some golf clubs and my wife a lawn mower!

I got my wife a new home perm waving outfit. I hit her over the head with a sheet of corrugated iron!

She bit into an apple and broke two teeth. I said, 'Don't get excited, love. You've still got one left.'

2/. T.V. Show

My wife said I saved myself for you – I said you didn't have to save so much. – She said I was Miss England – I said and a part of Wales too!!! She's on a diet, eats nothing but P. & B. all day long – hasn't lost weight – but you want to see her climb trees. A little boy said to me, the reason I like watching your show, is because as soon as it's over, a better one comes on!! Cutest Button Nose Gag. Russian Gag. Sunday Mirror Gag. Thursday Gag. Parrot Gag. This High From ground. Two Men Fighting in Rain.

My wife said, 'I saved myself for you.' I said, 'You didn't have to save so much.' She said, 'I was Miss England.' I said, 'And a part of Wales too!!'

TOMMY THE FILM STAR

'YOU'VE HEARD OF THE LONE RANGER? I'M HIS BROTHER, HYDRANGEA!'

When I was in Hollywood I made two pictures – face forward and sideways.

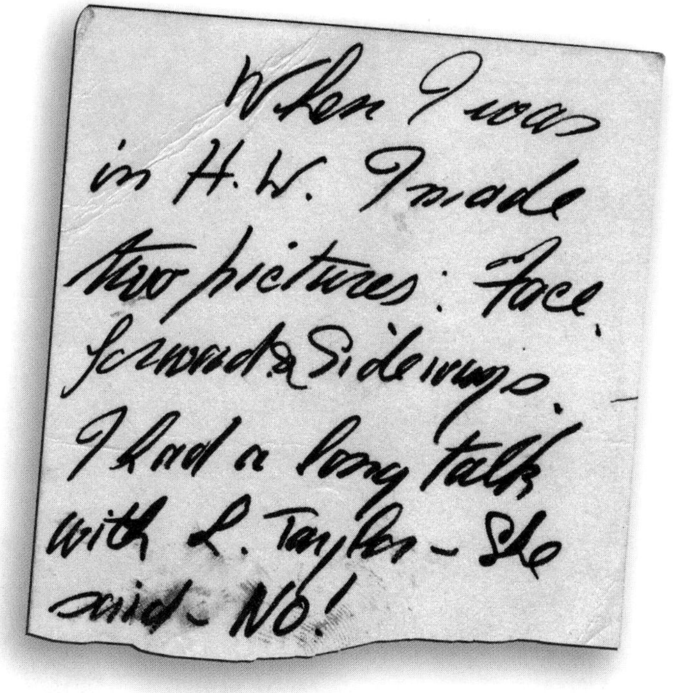
When I was
in H.W. I made
two pictures: face
forward & Sideways.
I had a long talk
with L. Taylor – she
said – NO!

While I was there I had a long talk with Elizabeth Taylor – she said, 'No!'

You know I've just been offered a part in a film. I have really. And it's a very sympathetic part – a very sympathetic part. I'll give you a rough idea of what it is. The scene opens like that. *(Tommy spreads out his arms)* There's a thatched cottage all made of thatch and there are a lot of violins going. *(He hums appropriate sound effects)* It'll be better than that – I'm just making it up! And there's a dear old lady in an armchair there and a dear old man sitting in an armchair there. There's a baby in the cot over there and a dog on the mat. And I have this very sympathetic part. I creep in through the door and hit the old man on the top of the head – see – and he doesn't say much. He just says, 'Ooh!' It isn't loud – just, 'Ooh!' Then I stab the lady in the back. She doesn't like it. Then I strangle the baby. Now this is where the sympathetic part comes in. On the way out I pat the dog!

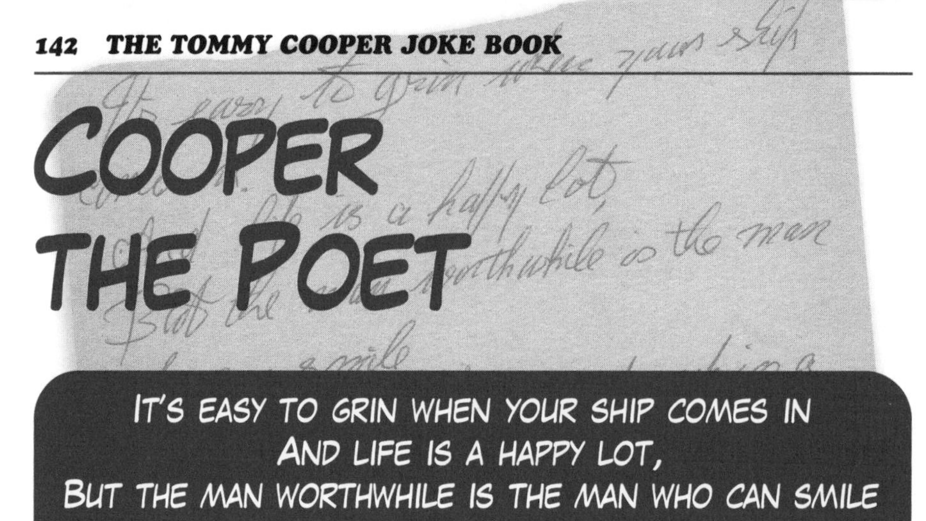

COOPER THE POET

IT'S EASY TO GRIN WHEN YOUR SHIP COMES IN
AND LIFE IS A HAPPY LOT,
BUT THE MAN WORTHWHILE IS THE MAN WHO CAN SMILE
WHEN HIS SHIRT CREEPS UP IN A KNOT.

HUMPTY DUMPTY SAT ON A WALL
HUMPTY DUMPTY HAD A GREAT FALL
ALL THE KING'S HORSES
AND ALL THE KING'S MEN SAID,
'OH, TO HELL WITH IT!'

THERE WAS A SCOTSMAN
NAMED ANDY.
HE WENT TO A PUB FOR A SHANDY.
HE BLEW OFF THE FROTH,
USED HIS KILT FOR A CLOTH,
AND THE BARMAN SAID,
'ANDY, THAT'S HANDY.'

I want no part of
outer space
Keep your moon and
star.
Give me one bit of
Inner space.
Where I can park
my car!!!

I WANT NO PART OF OUTER SPACE
KEEP YOUR MOON AND STAR
GIVE ME ONE BIT OF INNER SPACE
WHERE I CAN PARK MY CAR!

More Lucky Dip

PEOPLE ALWAYS ASK ME WHAT I'M LIKE OFF STAGE. WELL, I'VE GOT QUITE A FEW HOBBIES, YOU KNOW. ONE OF MY HOBBIES - I'M A COLLECTOR. I COLLECT DUST. AND I DO PAINTING TOO. YOU KNOW HOW PEOPLE PAINT BANANAS, ORANGES, AND APPLES? WELL, I PAINT THE JUICE!

DID YOU HEAR ABOUT THE MILLIONAIRE, WHO SAID TO HIS CHAUFFEUR, 'DRIVE OFF THE CLIFFS, JAMES. I'M COMMITTING SUICIDE'?

THIS OLD MAN SAID, 'I HAVEN'T TASTED FOOD FOR WEEKS.' I SAID, 'DON'T WORRY. IT STILL TASTES THE SAME.'

THERE'S A NEW KIND OF RUSSIAN ROULETTE - YOU GET SIX COBRAS IN A ROOM AND YOU PLAY A FLUTE. ONE OF THEM IS DEAF!'

TWO ZULUS WERE TALKING. ONE SAID, 'I DON'T LIKE MY WIFE.' THE OTHER SAID, 'WELL, JUST EAT THE VEGETABLES.'

I USED TO WASH MY HAIR IN VINEGAR. I DID. BUT I GAVE IT UP. THE CHIPS KEPT GETTING IN THE WAY!

I KNOCKED SOMEONE DOWN ON MY BIKE THE OTHER DAY. HE SAID, 'CAN'T YOU RING THE BELL?' I SAID, I CAN RING THE BELL - BUT I CAN'T RIDE THE BIKE!'

THIS WOMAN WENT TO THE DOCTOR. HE SAID, 'YOU'VE GOT A BAD BACK.' SHE SAID, 'I WANT A SECOND OPINION.' HE SAID, 'WELL, YOU'RE UGLY AS WELL.'

I WAS IN THIS HOTEL. I RANG DOWN TO THE MANAGER AND SAID, 'THERE'S NO CEILING TO MY ROOM.' HE SAID, 'THAT'S ALRIGHT. THE MAN ABOVE YOU DOESN'T WALK ABOUT MUCH.'

THIS GUY CAN'T STAND HEIGHTS. HE'S THE ONLY FELLOW I KNOW WHO TAKES ALONG A TANK OF OXYGEN TO PAINT THE LIVING ROOM CEILING.

I THINK THE MAID IS DISHONEST. I JUST FOUND OUT TWO OF THE TOWELS I SWIPED FROM A MANCHESTER HOTEL ARE MISSING.

SOMEBODY RANG MY WIFE AND SAID, 'I SAW YOUR HUSBAND ON THE BEACH WITH A BLONDE ON HIS ARM.' SHE SAID, 'WHAT DO YOU EXPECT AT HIS AGE - A BUCKET AND SPADE?'

LAST WEEK AN INSURANCE MANAGER CAME UP TO ME AND I SAID, 'I'M SORRY. I'VE GOT PLENTY OF INSURANCE.' HE SAID, 'NO, JUST LISTEN TO ME FIRST.' HE SAID, 'ARE YOU LISTENING?' I SAID, 'I AM.' I WAS! AND I LOOKED AT HIM LIKE THAT - SQUARE IN THE EYES - HE HAD SQUARE EYES! AND HE SAID, 'LOOK, YOU PAY TUPPENCE A WEEK FOR FIFTY YEARS. THAT'S ALL. AND WHEN YOU GET TO NINETY, YOU GET A HUNDRED POUNDS. I KNOW IT'S NOT MUCH, BUT IT'S A GREAT START IN LIFE.'

Tommy at the Wheel

FEZ 1

I call my car 'Flattery' – it gets me nowhere!

I just solved the parking problem – I bought a parked car!

We were bumper to bumper. I saw a fellow walking. I said, 'Would you like a lift?' He said, 'No thanks, I'm in a hurry.'

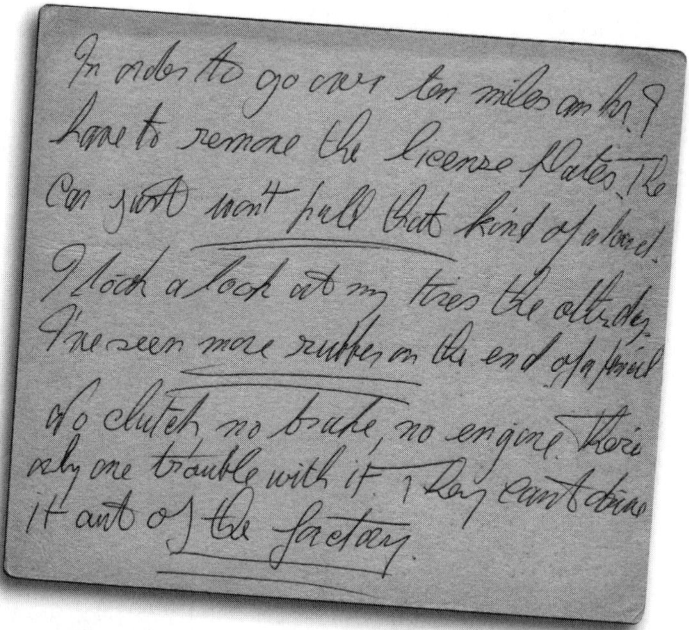
In order to go over ten miles an hr. I have to remove the license plates. The car just won't pull that kind of a load.
I took a look at my tires the other day. I've seen more rubber on the end of a pencil
No clutch, no brake, no engine. There's only one trouble with it. They can't drive it out of the factory.

In order to go over ten miles an hour I have to remove the license plates from my car. It just won't pull that kind of a load!

I took a look at my tyres the other day. I've seen more rubber on the end of a pencil.

My new car has no clutch, no brake, no engine. There's only one trouble with it. They can't drive it out of the factory.

I don't feel so good. I got in late last night and I rammed right into my garage doors. I even knocked one off. It's a good thing I didn't have the car!

Someone actually complimented me on my driving the other day. They put a note on my windscreen that said, 'Parking fine.' So that was nice.

COOPER CLASSIC 5

THIS LADY WENT TO THIS GREAT PAINTER AND SHE SAID TO THE PAINTER, 'I'D LIKE A PORTRAIT DONE OF MYSELF, A BIG ONE TO PUT IN MY HOUSE, SEE.' SHE SAID, 'I'VE HEARD YOU'RE VERY GOOD. I DON'T WANT YOU TO PUT ANY DIMPLES IN THAT AREN'T THERE. DON'T DO THAT. I WANT YOU TO CAPTURE ME EXACTLY AS I REALLY AM.' AND SHE SAID, 'IF YOU'VE GOT ANY PAINT LEFT OVER,' SHE SAID, 'WOULD YOU PAINT A DIAMOND AND RUBY NECKLACE ROUND MY THROAT LIKE THAT. NOT LIKE THAT. LIKE THAT. AND DIAMOND AND RUBY BRACELETS AND A DIAMOND AND RUBY RING AND A BIG TIARA.' AND THE PAINTER SAID, 'THAT WILL BE NO TROUBLE AT ALL.' HE SAID, 'BUT I'D LIKE TO KNOW WHY ARE YOU DOING THAT?' SHE SAID, 'WELL, I'LL TELL YOU WHAT, MY HUSBAND'S UP TO NO GOOD. AND WHEN HE MARRIES HIS SECOND WIFE, SHE'S EITHER GOING TO HAVE A NERVOUS BREAKDOWN OR DROP DOWN DEAD LOOKING FOR THE NECKLACE AND THE BRACELETS.' HUH HUH HUH!

COOPER BY ROYAL COMMAND

I'll never forget that Royal Variety Performance in the sixties. There I am standing in the line up on the stage of the London Palladium. They're all there. Jimmy Tarbuck, Cliff Richard, Lena Horne. And the Queen comes up to me. And she says, 'Oh, Mr. Cooper, you were really wonderful tonight, really you were.' And I went, 'Oh, thank you, ma'am. Did you laugh?' And she went, 'Oh yes, we all laughed.' And I said, 'That's good – then could I ask you something personal?' Well, the Queen, she looked at me – with her eyes – and she said, 'As personal as I'll allow.' And I said, 'Does your majesty like football?' She said, 'Not particularly.' And I said, 'Well, could I have your tickets for the Cup Final?'

The Hats Routine

No performance by Tommy Cooper was complete without his rendition of this classic routine, specially written by Val Andrews and Freddie Sadler soon after he became famous in the mid-fifties.

In this classic routine Tommy stands beside a table upon which rests a shabby cardboard box. The box is full of hats, which he puts on one at a time to illustrate the tale he has to tell, returning each one to the box before putting on the next, an inevitable blueprint for confusion and chaos.

I tell you what I'd like to do for you now if I may - I'd like to recite for you a poem. It's a love story - a sophisticated story along the lines of Noël Coward, in which I shall play every part and to clarify each character I play I wear different hats. And the poem is called 'New Year's Eve.'

It was New Year's Eve in Joe's Pub, a happy mob was there.

The bar and tables were crowded, lots of noise filled the air.

In the midst of all this gaiety the door banged open wide.

A torn and tattered tramp walked in.

'Happy New Year, folks,' he cried.

(Tommy puts on a floppy, felt Tramp's hat...)

The crowd just looked at him and laughed and some began to jeer,

(He replaces Tramp's hat with Sailor's hat...)

But a sailor standing at the bar said, 'Ship ahoy, mate, have a beer.'

(Back to Tramp's hat...)

'I thank you, sir,' the tramp replied, 'the beer and me are through.

I'll never touch a drop again, but I'll split a bottle of rum with you.'

(He now puts on a battered old Bowler hat...)

Then up jumped an old banker, who happened to be there,

'Throw that tramp out,' he cried,
'he contaminates the air.'

(Back to Sailor's hat...)

'Them's harsh words, friend,' the sailor said.

(Back to Bowler...)

The banker said,
'So what!'

(Next a Cowboy's Stetson...)

'Them's shooting words,' a cowboy said. 'Are you aimin' to be shot?'

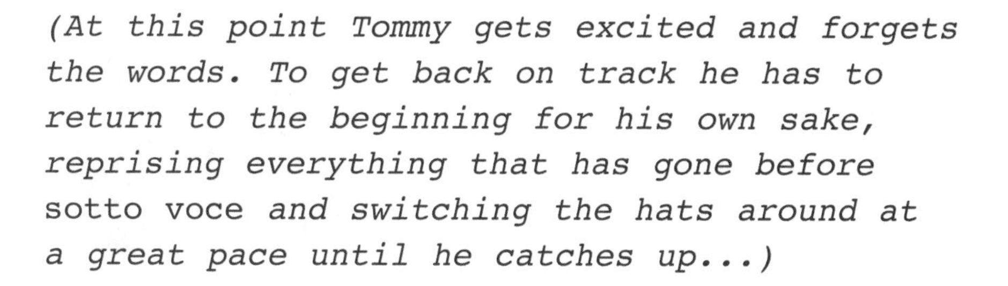

(At this point Tommy gets excited and forgets the words. To get back on track he has to return to the beginning for his own sake, reprising everything that has gone before sotto voce *and switching the hats around at a great pace until he catches up...)*

I won't be a minute.

(Eventually...)

Oh, yes!

(He puts on Soldier's hat...)

Then up jumped a soldier, who was standing at the bar,

'This ain't no time to fight.'

(Back to Sailor's hat...)

'You're right,' said the sailor...

(The Bowler...)

And the banker said,
'Well, all right.'

Then up jumped a woman

(He quickly produces a lady's bonnet – a hat that is funny in itself...)

And stared at the tramp.

'My goodness, it's Sam,' she cried with fright and her face went white.

(A Fireman's helmet...)

'Who's Sam?' a fireman asked,

(Tramp's hat...)

And the tramp pulled out a knife and said:

'I am Sam', he cried, 'and that painted woman once called herself my wife.'

(Stetson...)

'Don't stand for it,' the cowboy said.

(Soldier's hat...)

'Give me the knife,' the soldier cried.

(Fireman's helmet...)

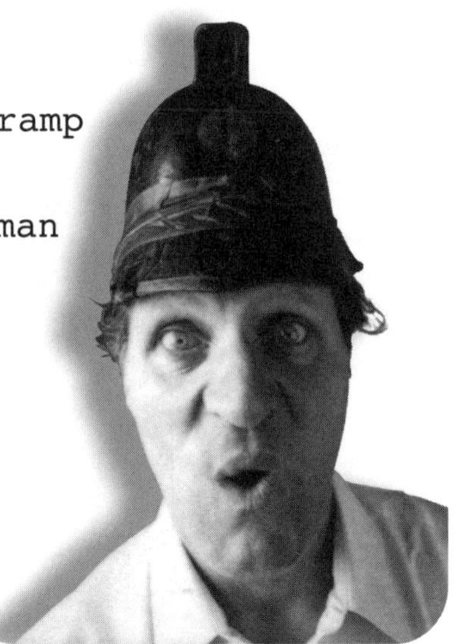

The fireman then hit the tramp

And said, 'That painted woman is my promised bride.'

(Tramp's hat...)

'Nuts, don't make me laugh,' the tramp replied,

'You cannot wed that horse.'

(Fireman's helmet...)

'Why not?' said the fireman.

(Tramp's hat...)

The tramp replied, 'We never were divorced.'

(Lady's bonnet...)

'It's a lie' the woman shouted.

(Tramp's hat...)

'It's the truth,' the tramp yelled out.

'Hold everything,' said the sailor,

(Tommy rummages for the Sailor's hat but can't immediately find it...)

I've got to get a bigger box! Where was I up to? Help me out. We're gonna be here all night! Oh - the sailor!

(The Sailor's hat...)

'Hold everything,' said the sailor,

'What the heck's it all about?'

(Bowler...)

'Who are you to but in?' the banker said.

(Stetson...)

The cowboy said, 'Shut up.'

(Soldier's hat...)

The soldier said, 'Hold it boys,'

And the fireman said...

(Tommy brings up the Fireman's helmet sharply and 'accidentally' hits himself with considerable force on the forehead. He registers pain and appeals to the wings...)

Now that is dangerous, that is. You should have padded that a bit. I could have cut my head open with that.

(He finishes putting on the helmet and resumes the poem...)

And the fireman said,
'I'll kill that pup.'

'Aaah...

(Searching again, he comes up with a Pilot's leather helmet...)

...A tough guy,' said the pilot...

(Tommy lifts the earflaps...)

I can't hear myself!

...Who was standing at the bar.

(Stetson...)

Then the cowboy hit the fireman,

(Fireman's helmet...)

And the fireman hit the floor.

He got up straightaway and looked at the woman and said, 'I was a mug for you to fall.'

And then he hit her.

'By gosh,' she screamed.

(Lady's bonnet...)

'Aaargh!'

And then the fight was free for all.

(Tight beret...)

In rushed a Frenchman.

(Cap...)

A little schoolboy.

(An Admiral's hat, which he slings to one side...)

I don't know who that is!

In the middle of all this fighting you could hear the knuckles crunch,

When all of a sudden they heard a policeman's whistle...

(No sound – he raises his voice...)

They heard a policeman's whistle...

(No sound – he raises his voice some more...)

They heard a policeman's whistle...

(At last we hear the sound of a whistle from the wings. Tommy surveys the stagehand with disdain...)

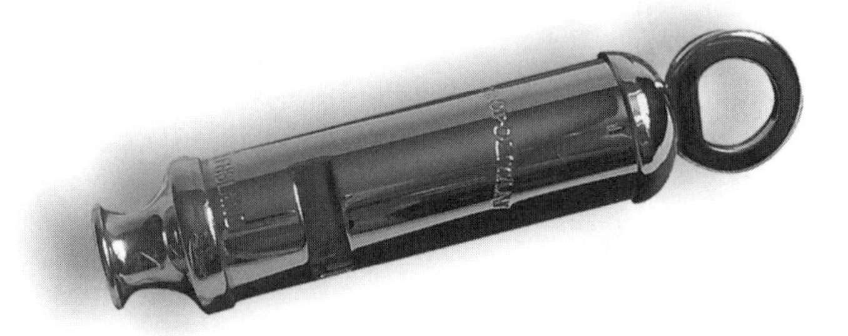

Isn't it marvellous, eh? That's all he has to do. And he's wearing make-up as well!

(He finally puts on a Policeman's helmet...)

And then a policeman came in and pinched the whole damn bunch!

Thank you very much. Goodnight!

A Last Roundup

Just before the show the producer took me to one side and left me there! He came back and he said, 'How do you feel tonight?' I said, 'A little bit funny.' He said, 'Well, get out there before it wears off.'

I met this man at the airport. He said, 'Would you like to share a taxi with me?' I said, 'Okay.' He said, 'You take the wheels, I'll take the engine.'

This man sat next to me on the plane. He said, 'I've got a parrot at home that says, "Who's a pretty boy, then? Who's a pretty boy?"' I said, 'Well, what's so special about that? A lot of parrots say, "Who's a pretty boy? Who's a pretty boy?"' He said, 'Yes, but this one's stuffed.'

Our dog was rubbing two sticks together. My little boy said, 'What's he trying to tell us, dad?' I said, 'He's trying to tell us he wants to join the boy scouts!'

One kangaroo said to the other, 'I hope it doesn't rain. I hate it when the kids have to play inside!'

The other week I had to share my dressing room with a monkey. The producer came in and said, 'I'm sorry about this.' I said, 'That's okay.' He said, 'I wasn't talking to you.'

'THANK YOU VERY MUCH!'

ACKNOWLEDGEMENTS

I would like to thank Tommy's daughter, Vicky Cooper and John Miles, on behalf of the Tommy Cooper Estate, for their gracious cooperation in the preparation of this volume. Special acknowledgment is also made to Val Andrews, Eddie Bayliss, Peter Cagney, Simon Callow, Gwen Cooper, Beatrice Ferrie, Miff Ferrie, Jerome Flynn, Eddie Gay, Billy Glason, David Hemingway, Sir Anthony Hopkins, Peter Hudson, Tudor Jones and the members of the Tommy Cooper Appreciation Society, Mary Kay, Gershon Legman, Jay Marshall, Max Miller, Sir Spike Milligan, Bob Monkhouse, Robert Orben, Art Paul, Patrick Ryecart, Freddie Sadler and Jerry Seinfeld.

Trevor Dolby, at Preface, had the foresight to see how Tommy Cooper could make us laugh again on the printed page and I extend my thanks to him and his editorial team headed by Nicola Taplin and Neil Bradford. While every effort has been made to trace the owners of copyright material produced herein, the publishers would like to apologise for any omissions and will be pleased to incorporate missing acknowledgments in future editions, provided that notification is made to them in writing.

The volume would be only half of what it is without the flair and dedication brought to its conception and design by Andy Spence, to whom I extend my deepest gratitude. As always, I also owe a major debt of thanks to my representative, Charles Armitage and his associate, Di Evans. The loving support of my wife, Sue, goes without saying.